DESSERTS

DESSERTS

ACHIEVABLE, SATISFYING SWEET TREATS

Project Editor Siobhán O'Connor
Project Designer Alison Shackleton
Editor Kiron Gill
US Editor Nathalie Mornu
US Consultant Renee Wilmeth
Jacket Designer Alison Donovan
Jackets Coordinator Jasmin Lennie
Production Editor David Almond
Production Controller Denitsa Kenanska
Managing Editor Dawn Henderson
Managing Art Editor Alison Donovan
Art Director Maxine Pedliham
Publishing Director Katie Cowan

First American Edition, 2022
Published in the United States by DK Publishing
1450 Broadway, Suite 801, New York, NY 10018

Copyright © 2022 Dorling Kindersley Limited
DK, a Division of Penguin Random House LLC
22 23 24 25 26   10 9 8 7 6 5 4 3 2 1
001–327875–Aug/2022

A catalog record for this book is available from the Library of Congress.
ISBN 978-0-7440-5684-6

DK books are available at special discounts when purchased in bulk for sales
promotions, premiums, fund-raising, or educational use. For details, contact:
DK Publishing Special Markets,
1450 Broadway, Suite 801, New York, NY 10018
SpecialSales@dk.com

Printed and bound in China

For the curious
www.dk.com

This book was made with Forest Stewardship Council ™ certified paper—
one small step in DK's commitment to a sustainable future.
For more information go to **www.dk.com/our-green-pledge**.

Contents

Desserts

For most of us today, desserts are treats to be relished when we're eating out, have guests over, or gather for a special family meal, rather than something we eat every day. All the more applause for the cook, then, when something sweet and beautiful appears to crown the meal.

The recipes in this book are innovative twists on classics. Some are simple and quick to put together, while others are more time-consuming—extravagant offerings to impress on a special occasion, but well worth the effort. With so many tempting choices, narrowing down what to make can be a conundrum for anyone with a sweet tooth. With this in mind, for ease of choice we have grouped the recipes in this book according to flavor combinations, many of which have a seasonal bent, with a final chapter for especially festive occasions, when you want to pull out all the stops.

Fresh and fruity

In this chapter citrus, berries, passion fruit, and stone fruit all reign supreme. There are also more exotic fruits, such as mango, figs, and pomegranate. It may seem that nothing could exceed the appeal of a perfectly ripe piece of fresh fruit—but what about a luscious meringue stack filled with a tangy lemon and passion fruit cream and topped with raspberries?

Let your choices be led by the fruit that is in season, as this will provide the best-tasting dessert. Embrace fruit that corresponds with cooking methods that suit the time of year, too. In cooler months, seek out baked treats, such as sweetly satisfying apple, blackberry, and marzipan pies or a clafoutis of late-season berries, or enjoy the comfort that only a warm muffin or cake brings. If the sun is shining and the weather is warm, opt for something lighter and fresher. Granitas and perfectly ripe fruits layered with cream are good choices, and gelatin-based desserts such as panna cotta have a distinct advantage: They can be prepared well in advance.

Chocolate and coffee

These two ingredients conjure up tempting visions of richness and indulgence. Depending on the cooking method, the texture and intensity of flavor can be altered. A chocolate–egg base, lightened with egg whites, becomes a light-as-air soufflé. For lovers of rich chocolate desserts, we offer up a molten lava cake, fig-laden brownies, and churros, the Spanish fried pastry in which crisp lengths of pastry are unabashedly dipped in a rich chocolate sauce. Coffee and chocolate make good bedfellows, too, enhancing each other's flavors, so in this chapter you will see them in company as well as alone.

Nuts and caramel

Even with only eight nuts at your command, a world of possibilities opens. Nuts left whole and toasted provide texture within desserts, as well as adding depth to their flavor profile. Ground to a flour they yield muffins, cakes, crumble toppings, and cookies that look marvelous but are surprisingly simple to make. Caramel is the alchemy that happens by cooking sugar and water to a burnished golden hue; the process of caramelization dissipates the sweetness of sugar, developing complex aromas and flavors that can be buttery, sour, nutty, malty, or toasty. Caramels that include butter and cream become butterscotch and add still more richness and mouthfeel. Nuts and caramel can stand as sweet confections all on their own, too—think crunchy cinnamon-spiced almonds or home-made caramels that range from simple fudge to more sophisticated candies with intriguing flavor twists. Premade caramel sauces such as dulce de leche are featured here, too, adding their own stamp in flavor and texture combinations designed to entice.

Spices and herbs

Spices and herbs have been making their way along spice and trade routes and into various cuisines since ancient times. Fragrant vanilla, the world's favorite flavoring, is of course used throughout the book, but you will find it united with other flavors such as basil, rosemary, and even chili. Infusing milk or cream-based desserts is another simple way to add interesting flavor notes. And spices are one of the easiest ways to add different sparks of flavor. Sweet treats with spices complement a menu with a Mediterranean or Middle Eastern bent perfectly.

Special occasions

One of the deepest pleasures of festive events are the traditional desserts that have become an essential and time-honored part of the entire occasion. They may belong wholly to a particular festival or tradition, like a Yule log, or they might appear at other times of the year to mark important occasions such as summer graduations or family gatherings. They could be a tradition closer to home, like the special treat chosen for birthdays. All of these family gatherings feature desserts treasured for what they mean beyond just the pleasure of eating them: continuity, togetherness, the assurance that some things never change. Or do they? Lots of people who celebrate Christmas will think of fruit cake or of baking special cookies in the week before the holiday—but the idea of having a frozen dessert or other cake has caught on quickly, and today it has become a tradition parallel to the old ones. It's called enjoying the best of both worlds.

And so, the result is this beautiful collection of sweet treats and heady desserts. Go ahead and indulge—and impress yourself, your family, and your friends.

FRESH AND FRUITY

From delectable tarts and puddings bursting with flavor to frozen treats and cheesecakes perfect for the lazy days of summer, these desserts showcase the best of seasonal fruit.

Ruby red slab tart

BAKED AND FRESH | PREP + COOK TIME **45 MINUTES + REFRIGERATION** | SERVES **8**

A slab tart is an easy and not-at-all-intimidating dessert for a novice baker to make, as it eliminates some of the elements that may cause grief. As an added bonus, it also requires no specific bakeware—a boon in the repertoire of any baker, regardless of skill level.

1¹/₃ cups flour

2 tbsp cocoa powder

2 tbsp powdered sugar

¹/₂ cup + 3 tbsp cold butter, chopped

about 2 tbsp iced water

1¹/₄ cups coconut yogurt (see tips)

¹/₂ cup watermelon, peeled into thin slices

3 fresh figs, cut into wedges

8 strawberries, halved

4oz (125g) raspberries

1 tbsp pomegranate seeds (see tips)

glaze

1 cup pomegranate juice

2 tbsp cranberry sauce

1 tbsp honey

1 Preheat the oven to 350°F (180°C).

2 In the bowl of a food processor, combine the flour, cocoa powder, powdered sugar, and butter. Pulse until the mixture forms coarse crumbs. With the motor operating, add just enough of the iced water for the dough to come together. Turn onto a clean work surface. Shape into a rectangle. Wrap the dough in plastic wrap. Refrigerate for 20 minutes.

3 Roll out the pastry between sheets of parchment paper into a ¹/₄in (5mm) thick oval that measures 6in x 12in (15cm x 30cm). Discard the top sheet of parchment paper. Transfer the pastry, still on the parchment, to a baking sheet. Bake for 12 minutes or until cooked through. Let cool to room temperature.

4 Meanwhile, to make the pomegranate glaze, combine the ingredients in a small saucepan over high heat. Bring to a boil. Boil for 10 minutes or until reduced to a syrupy consistency.

5 Spread the yogurt over the pastry, leaving a ¹/₂in (1cm) border. Top with the fruit and pomegranate seeds. Drizzle with the pomegranate glaze.

TIPS

• Instead of using coconut yogurt, spread the tart with mascarpone, if you like.

• To remove the seeds from a pomegranate, cut the fruit in half. Hold a half, skin-side up, over a large, deep bowl. While squeezing the fruit slightly, use a wooden spoon to tap the skin vigorously to release the seeds. Continue until all of the seeds are released, then remove any white pith that may have fallen into the bowl.

• To prevent the pastry from softening, assemble the tart close to serving.

Lemon and passion fruit pavlova stack

BAKED/ASSEMBLED | PREP + COOK TIME **1 HOUR 45 MINUTES + COOLING** | SERVES **10**

This impressive-looking dessert is a meltingly light confection of crisp and soft meringue.
The lemon curd, raspberries, and passion fruit cut through the sweetness of the
meringue, lending freshness and acidity for a perfect balance of flavors.

6 egg whites

pinch of cream of tartar

1^1/$_2$ cups sugar

3 tsp cornstarch, sifted

2 tsp vanilla bean paste or vanilla extract

1^1/$_2$ tsp white vinegar

8oz (225g) fresh raspberries

lemon passion fruit cream

2^1/$_2$ cups whipping cream

^{2}/$_3$ cup lemon curd (see tips)

^{1}/$_2$ cup passion fruit pulp (see tips)

meringue cones

^{3}/$_4$ cup sugar

3 egg whites

TIPS

• You'll find lemon curd in the specialty aisle of
your grocery store, or near the jams and jellies.
• Look for passion fruit pulp in the freezer section
of the market or at Mexican or international
groceries. If you like, you can omit folding the
pulp into the cream and spoon it over the cream
layers instead.
• The pavlovas can be baked a day ahead; store
them in an airtight container in a cool, dry place.
• The pavlovas are quite delicate. Use 2 large metal
spatulas to lift and move them.
• This recipe is best assembled close to serving.

1 To make the pavlova bases, preheat the oven to 250°F (120°C). Grease
two 9in (20cm) springform cake pans and line the bottoms with
baking parchment.

2 Using an electric mixer, whisk the egg whites and cream of tartar until
soft peaks form. Gradually add the sugar, beating after each addition,
until the sugar has dissolved and the mixture is thick and glossy and
forms stiff peaks. Fold in the cornstarch, then the vanilla and vinegar.

3 Divide the meringue between the prepared pans; smooth the tops. Bake
for 1 hour or until dry to the touch and slightly brown on top. Turn off the
oven. Let the pavlovas cool completely in the oven with the door ajar
before carefully removing the collars from the pans.

4 Meanwhile, to make the lemon passion fruit cream, using an electric
mixer, whip the whipping cream in a bowl until firm peaks form. Fold it
through the lemon curd and passion fruit pulp. Refrigerate until needed.

5 To stack, carefully place 1 pavlova on a plate. Top with three-quarters of
the lemon passion fruit cream. Sprinkle with half of the raspberries. Top
with the remaining pavlova. Spoon over the remaining cream.

6 To make the meringue cones, stir the sugar and ^{1}/$_4$ cup water in a small
saucepan over low heat until the sugar dissolves. Increase the heat to
high. Bring to a boil. Boil, without stirring, for 4 minutes or until the syrup
reaches 244°F (118°C) (soft-ball stage) on a candy thermometer (or until
a small amount of syrup dropped into ice-cold water can be rolled into a
soft, pliable ball). Using an electric mixer, beat the egg whites in a bowl
until soft peaks form. Gradually beat in the hot sugar syrup. Beat for
5 minutes more or until cooled to room temperature.

7 Preheat the broiler to high. Drop 2 tablespoons of mixture at a time onto
a parchment-lined baking sheet, forming peaks. Broil for 30 seconds or
until lightly browned. Gently transfer the meringue cones onto the
pavlova stack. Serve sprinkled with the remaining raspberries.

Roasted plums with rose water

SET | PREP + COOK TIME **45 MINUTES** | SERVES **4**

Rose water adds a touch of elegance to any dessert, and these plums are delightfully tender, sweet, and floral. You could use other stone fruit, such as apricots or nectarines, if you prefer. The dense texture of pound cake makes it easier to slice into cubes than sponge.

6 small plums, halved and quartered

½ cup sugar

1 tbsp rose water (see tips)

1 tsp vanilla bean paste (see tips)

½ lb (225g) premade pound cake, cut into 1in (2.5cm) cubes (see tips)

4 tbsp butter, melted

1 cup whipping cream

2 tbsp powdered sugar

¼ cup coarsely chopped pistachios

2 tbsp fresh raspberries

1 tbsp dried edible rose buds, optional (see tips)

1   Preheat the oven to 425°F (220°C).

2   Gently combine the plums, sugar, rose water, and vanilla in a large bowl. Spoon the mixture into a shallow baking dish. Roast for 15 minutes or until tender, turning the plums halfway through the cooking time.

3   Meanwhile, combine the cake and butter in a medium bowl. Arrange the cake pieces in a single layer on a baking sheet. Bake for 10 minutes, turning halfway through the cooking time, or until golden.

4   Using an electric mixer, beat together the whipping cream and powdered sugar in a medium bowl until soft peaks form.

5   Divide the whipped cream among 4 serving bowls; drizzle with a little syrup from the plums. Top with the roasted plums, buttered cake pieces, pistachios, raspberries, and dried rose buds, if you like.

TIPS

- You'll find rose water in Middle Eastern groceries or in the specialty food aisle of your market. Buy dried edible rose buds at specialty food stores.
- You can substitute the same amount of vanilla extract for vanilla bean paste.
- If you bake your own pound cake instead of buying it, you can make it a day ahead.
- The roasted plums and buttered cake cubes can be prepared several hours ahead of serving.

Coconut banana fritters

FRIED | PREP + COOK TIME **30 MINUTES** | SERVES **4**

Using panko breadcrumbs instead of regular breadcrumbs or crushed-up cookies gives these fritters an extra crunchy shell to bite into when you eat them. The textural sensation provides a wonderful contrast to the softness of the banana in the middle.

$^1/_4$ cup powdered sugar

2 tsp ground cinnamon

1 egg

$^3/_4$ cup panko breadcrumbs

$^1/_4$ cup shredded coconut

vegetable oil for deep-frying

4 large bananas, halved lengthwise

2 cups ice cream or gelato with coconut flakes (see tips)

1 Combine the powdered sugar and cinnamon in a shallow bowl. Lightly whisk the egg in another shallow bowl. Combine the breadcrumbs and coconut in a third shallow bowl.

2 Fill a large saucepan or wok with vegetable oil until it is one-third full. Heat to 350°F (180°C), or until a cube of bread dropped into the oil sizzles and browns in 15 seconds.

3 To make the fritters, first dip the bananas in the powdered sugar mixture; shake off any excess. Next, dip in the egg mixture, then lastly in the crumb mixture to coat. Deep-fry the bananas, in batches, for 2 minutes or until the coating is golden. Drain the fritters on paper towels.

4 Serve the hot fritters with scoops of the ice cream.

TIPS

- To make your own ice cream or gelato with coconut flakes, soften 2 cups high-quality vanilla ice cream or gelato, then fold in $^1/_2$ cup toasted shredded coconut and 1 tbsp coconut-flavored liqueur. Return to the freezer until firm enough to scoop.
- You can use yogurt with shredded coconut instead of the ice cream, if you like.

Strawberry "jellies" with snowballs

FRESH AND FROZEN | PREP + COOK TIME **1 HOUR 10 MINUTES + REFRIGERATION + FREEZING** | MAKES **6**

Choose the ripest, most fragrant strawberries to make the most of this double infusion of their heavenly flavor. Pimm's is a classic British liqueur that infuses spices and herbs in a gin base. It's a perfect compliment to refreshing summer fruit.

2lb (1kg) strawberries, thinly sliced

$^2/_3$ cup sugar

$^1/_3$ cup Pimm's No. 1 Cup liqueur

8 gelatin leaves

2 cups vanilla ice cream

2oz (57g) meringue cookies, crushed

2 tsp dried pink peppercorns, crushed (optional)

macerated strawberries

8oz (250g) fresh strawberries, sliced $^1/_8$in (3mm) thick

1 tbsp sugar

2 tsp lemon juice

1 Put the strawberries, sugar, and Pimm's in a large heatproof bowl. Cover tightly with 2 layers of plastic wrap. Place the bowl over a large saucepan of simmering water. Heat for 40 minutes.

2 Place a large strainer over another large bowl. Strain the strawberry mixture through the strainer. Allow it to drip; don't press the mixture down, as this will make the liquid cloudy.

3 In a small saucepan, bring $^2/_3$ cup water to a simmer. Remove from the heat. Meanwhile, place the gelatin leaves in a bowl of cold water for 5 minutes. Squeeze out any excess water from the gelatin leaves, then add the gelatin to the pan of hot water. Stir to dissolve. Next, add the gelatin mixture to the strawberry liquid. Stir well to combine. Divide the unset gelatin evenly among six $1^1/_4$-cup glasses. Refrigerate, covered, for at least 4 hours or overnight until the jellies are set.

4 To make the snowballs, put a metal tray in the freezer. Scoop out 6 small balls of the ice cream. Put the crushed meringue cookies in a shallow bowl. Roll the ice cream balls in the meringue to coat them with cookie. Place the snowballs on the chilled metal tray. Cover with plastic wrap. Freeze until needed.

5 To make the macerated strawberries, combine the ingredients in a bowl. Let stand for 10 minutes.

6 Spoon the macerated strawberries over the jellies. Top each one with a snowball. Sprinkle with the crushed pink peppercorns, if you like.

TIPS

- If you have the time, the strawberries used in step 1 can be held at room temperature for 2 hours, instead of being heated.
- The strawberry pulp left in the strainer in step 2 can be added to smoothies or drinks, or puréed to add to fruit sauces.
- The jellies can be made a day ahead.
- The snowballs can be prepared up to 4 hours in advance.
- The strawberries for the macerated strawberries can be sliced 4 hours ahead. Add sugar and juice 10 minutes before serving.

Lime and mango semifreddo

FROZEN | PREP + COOK TIME 20 MINUTES + STANDING + OVERNIGHT FREEZING | SERVES 12

As it is essentially a frozen mousse, semifreddo has a lighter texture than ice cream and is often more subtly flavored as well. This makes it a refreshing end to a meal, particularly a substantial one, and this example with its tropical notes is no exception.

1½ cups whipping cream

4 eggs, separated

1/3 cup lime juice

1/2 cup sugar

2 small mangoes, peeled, thinly sliced (see tips)

macadamia nut praline

1/4 cup sugar

1 cup unsalted macadamia nuts, roasted, coarsely chopped (see tips)

1/2 cup flaked coconut, toasted

1   Lightly grease a 3in x 13in (8cm x 33cm) straight-sided loaf pan or terrine mold. Line it with plastic wrap, extending the wrap 4in (10cm) over the long sides. Line a large baking sheet with parchment paper.

2   To make the macadamia nut praline, heat the sugar in a medium nonstick skillet over medium-high heat for 2 minutes until bubbling and caramelized. Stir in the macadamia nuts. Cook for 1 minute longer or until the nuts are hot and well coated. Spread the nuts in a single layer on the parchment-lined baking sheet. Set aside for 10 minutes or until cooled and firm.

3   Break the macadamia nut praline into large pieces. Reserve a quarter of the pieces for serving, storing them in an airtight container in a cool, dry place until needed. Pulse the remaining praline with the coconut in a food processor until finely ground. Set aside.

4   Using an electric mixer, beat the whipping cream in a medium bowl until soft peaks form.

5   In a separate medium bowl, beat together the egg yolks, lime juice, and sugar with an electric mixer until pale and creamy.

6   Whisk the egg whites in a separate large bowl with an electric mixer until stiff peaks form.

7   Gently fold the egg yolk mixture into the whipped cream mixture. Fold in the egg whites. Fold in the ground praline mixture until just combined; do not overmix. Spoon the mixture into the lined pan; smooth the surface. Fold the overhanging plastic wrap over the mixture to cover. Freeze for 8 hours or overnight until firm.

8   To serve, let the semifreddo stand at room temperature for 20 minutes before lifting the plastic wrap out of the mold and transferring the dessert onto a platter. Decorate with the mango slices and reserved praline pieces.

TIPS

• Instead of mango, you can use another seasonal fresh fruit, such as berries or figs, if you like. You can also use thawed frozen fruit.

• Instead of using macadamia nuts for the praline, try almonds or cashews.

• The semifreddo can be made up to 1 week ahead. Store, covered, in the freezer.

Pomegranate and frozen yogurt cheesecakes

FROZEN | PREP + COOK TIME **40 MINUTES + FREEZING** | MAKES **4**

This recipe turns simple pre-purchased ingredients into an attractive and enticing dessert—
all with very little effort. Frozen yogurt adds tartness to the creamy filling. The tartness is
offset by fresh berries and tart-sweet pomegranate juice.

$3/4$ lb (350g) crispy butter cookies

5 tbsp butter, melted, plus extra for greasing

2 cups pomegranate seeds (see tips)

8oz (226g) cream cheese, room temperature

$1/2$ cup sugar

4 cups vanilla frozen yogurt

4oz (125g) fresh blackberries

micro basil, optional, to garnish

TIPS

- You will need about 2 large pomegranates for this recipe. Alternatively, purchase prepared pomegranate seeds from the produce department of your supermarket.
- To remove the seeds from a whole pomegranate, cut the pomegranate in half crosswise. Hold it in the palm of your hand over a bowl, cut-side down, then hit the outside firmly with a wooden spoon. The seeds should fall out easily; discard any white pith in the bowl. Scrape out any remaining seeds.
- Pomegranate seeds can be refrigerated in an airtight container for up to 4 days.
- The cheesecakes can be made to the end of step 4 up to a week ahead.
- Instead of making the pomegranate juice yourself, use $1/2$ cup purchased pomegranate juice instead.

1 Grease the bases of 6 individual 5in (13cm) springform pans with butter. Line the bottom of each pan with parchment paper.

2 Put the cookies in a zip-top bag. Using a rolling pin or meat mallet, crush the cookies into coarse crumbs. Shake the crumbs in a coarse strainer to remove any fine crumbs; discard. Put the large crumbs in a medium bowl. Stir in the melted butter. Press about $1/3$ cup of crumbs over the bottom of each prepared pan, pressing lightly to level. Freeze while preparing the filling.

3 Pulse 1 cup of the pomegranate seeds in a food processor until finely chopped. Reserve the rest to garnish. Strain the processed seeds through a strainer over a measuring cup to yield $1/2$ cup juice. In a large bowl, mix the cream cheese, sugar, and pomegranate juice until smooth. Add the frozen yogurt. Mix until combined. Freeze for 20 minutes or until firm but still able to be scooped.

4 Divide the mixture evenly among the prepared cake pans. Smooth the tops. Cover tightly with plastic wrap. Freeze for 4 hours or overnight until firm.

5 Remove the frozen cheesecakes from the cake pans. Decorate with the remaining pomegranate seeds, blackberries, and micro basil, if using.

Roasted pineapple with rum syrup

ROASTED | PREP + COOK TIME **1 HOUR 45 MINUTES** | SERVES **4**

Pineapple, rum, and lime form a classic trio of tropical flavors. One bite will transport you straight to a Caribbean island! Serve this dessert with vanilla or butterscotch ice cream, if you like, and you'll find it hard to let go of the culinary fantasy.

3 lbs (1.8kg) fresh pineapple spears, core and juice reserved

6 whole star anise (see tips)

$^3/_4$ cup sugar

1 cup dark rum, divided

7 tbsp butter, chopped

2 tbsp fresh mint leaves, to garnish

2 limes, cut into wedges, for serving

1   Preheat the oven to 400°F (200°C). Line a large baking sheet with parchment paper.

2   Thread the pineapple pieces onto metal skewers. Pat the pineapple dry with paper towels. Reserve any trimmed pieces.

3   Preheat a cast iron ridged grill pan or barbecue grill to high heat. Cook the pineapple skewers for 1 minute on each side or until grill marks appear. Transfer the pineapple to the lined baking sheet; set aside.

4   Crush the star anise using a mortar and pestle (or place it on a clean surface and press the base of a clean saucepan down onto it to crush it). Put in a medium heavy-based saucepan with the sugar, $^1/_4$ cup water, and the reserved juice, cores, and any trimmed pieces. Cook over low heat, stirring, until the sugar has dissolved. Increase the heat to medium. Cook, without stirring, for 15 minutes or until a golden brown caramel forms; as soon as the color begins to change, stir the caramel to ensure you don't overcook it.

5   Taking care, as the mixture will splutter, add $^3/_4$ cup of the rum to the caramel. Increase the heat to high. Boil for 2 minutes or until syrupy. Add the butter and 1 cup water. Boil for 10 minutes until thick. Add the remaining $^1/_4$ cup rum. Cook for 2 minutes longer. Strain into a heatproof bowl. Discard the solids.

6   Brush the grilled pineapple with the rum caramel syrup, reserving any leftover syrup. Roast the pineapple in the oven, basting with syrup every 10 minutes, for 45 minutes or until tender and caramelized. Let cool briefly on the baking sheet.

7   To serve, drizzle the pineapple skewers with the roasting juices and any remaining syrup. Sprinkle with the mint leaves, and serve with the lime cheeks for squeezing over.

TIPS

- Whole star anise is available in the spice aisle of supermarkets. You can use cinnamon instead.
- Serve with vanilla or butterscotch ice cream.

Lemon sherbet granita

FROZEN | PREP + COOK TIME **10 MINUTES + COOLING + FREEZING** | SERVES **4**

Granitas do not usually contain dairy products, so this ice confection is more of a hybrid, lying somewhere between a sherbet and a simple lemon granita—hence the name. It's easy to make and, with its zesty lemoniness, has wonderful palate-cleansing properties.

1 cup sugar

2 lemons

$^1/_2$ cup whipping cream

strips of lemon zest, to garnish

1 Stir the sugar and $2^1/_4$ cups water in a medium saucepan over low heat until the sugar dissolves.

2 Finely grate the zest of the lemons; you will need 1 tablespoon. Add the zest to the hot syrup. Let cool. Squeeze $^1/_2$ cup lemon juice from the lemons. Add to the syrup with the cream; mix well to combine.

3 Pour into an 8in x 12in (20cm x 30cm) rectangular cake or brownie pan, or some other shallow metal container.

4 Freeze for 2 hours. Use a fork to break up any ice crystals. Freeze for 9 hours longer, scraping with a fork every 3 hours or until frozen. Serve topped with strips of lemon zest.

Granita variations

Originally from Sicily, the granita is an integral element of Italy's love affair with frozen desserts—gelato, sorbetto ... the list goes on. The name comes from its grainy texture, which is achieved by running a fork through the flavored syrup base during the freezing process.

Cucumber, mint, and lime granita

Stir $3/4$ cup sugar and $1^1/2$ cups water in a medium saucepan over low heat until the sugar dissolves. Let cool. In a food processor, pulse $3/4$ lb (390g) European or Lebanese cucumbers, $1/2$ cup water, and 1 cup mint leaves until smooth. Strain through a fine strainer into a large heatproof bowl. Add the cooled syrup and $1/4$ cup of lime juice. Mix well. Pour into an 8in x 12in (20cm x 30cm) rectangular cake pan or shallow metal container. Freeze as instructed in step 4 of the lemon sherbet granita on page 26.

Pineapple and strawberry granita

Stir $3/4$ cup sugar and $1½$ cups water in a medium saucepan over low heat until the sugar dissolves. Let cool. In a food processor, pulse 8oz (225g) of fresh trimmed strawberries and 1 cup of pineapple juice until smooth. Add the strawberry mixture to a large heatproof bowl with the syrup and $1/4$ cup lemon juice. Pour into an 8in x 12in (20cm x 30cm) rectangular cake pan or shallow metal container. Freeze as instructed in step 4 of the lemon sherbet granita on page 26.

Nectarine and raspberry granita

Stir $3/4$ cup sugar and $1^1/2$ cups water in a medium saucepan over low heat until the sugar dissolves. Let cool. Pour into a large heatproof bowl. Meanwhile, in a food processor, pulse 4 chopped ripe white nectarines (pits removed), 4oz (125g) raspberries, and $1/4$ cup lemon juice until smooth. Strain the nectarine mixture through a fine strainer into the large heatproof bowl with the syrup. Pour into an 8in x 12in (20cm x 30cm) rectangular cake pan or shallow metal container. Freeze as instructed in step 4 of the lemon sherbet granita on page 26.

Passion fruit and elderflower granita

Stir $3/4$ cup sugar and $1^1/2$ cups water in a medium saucepan over low heat until the sugar dissolves. Let cool. Combine the syrup with $1^1/2$ cups elderflower cordial, 1 cup passion fruit pulp, and $1/4$ cup freshly squeezed lemon juice in a large bowl. Pour into an 8in x 12in (20cm x 30cm) rectangular cake pan or other shallow metal container. Freeze as instructed in step 4 of the lemon sherbet granita on page 26.

Apple, blackberry, and marzipan turnovers33

BAKED | PREP + COOK TIME **40 MINUTES** | MAKES **4**

These individual pies are pleasure in an edible parcel. The pairing of apples and blackberries is a classic one that is hard to beat. Use all-butter puff pastry for an extra decadent flavor and texture, and serve the pies topped with whipped cream, if you like.

1 large Granny Smith apple, cored, peeled, and chopped into ½in (1cm) pieces

2 tbsp sugar, divided

1 cup frozen blackberries

1 tsp cornstarch

3oz (80g) marzipan, finely chopped (see tips)

2 sheets of frozen puff pastry

1 Preheat the oven to 350°F (180°C). Line two baking sheets with parchment paper.

2 Put the apple in a bowl with the blackberries, 1 tablespoon of the sugar, the corn starch, and marzipan. Stir well to combine, ensuring the fruit is evenly coated in both sugar and cornstarch.

3 Cut the pastry sheets in half. Place one-quarter of the fruit mixture on one half of each pastry rectangle, leaving a border on all sides. Fold the opposite end over to enclose the fruit. Press the edges together with a fork to seal. Place the pies on the lined baking sheets. Cut three slits across the top of each one. Brush lightly with water. Sprinkle with the remaining sugar.

4 Bake the pies for 25 minutes or until the pastry is puffed and golden. Serve warm.

TIPS

- Marzipan is an almond paste that you'll find in the baking aisle.
- You can use other frozen berries instead of blackberries. Raspberries, mixed berries, and cherries would all work well here.

Plum and mascarpone tart

BAKED | PREP + COOK TIME **1 HOUR 40 MINUTES + REFRIGERATION** | SERVES **10**

Either moscato or an ice wine would work well in this recipe. The key to cooking with wine—
which is used here to poach the plums—is never to cook with anything that you wouldn't
actually enjoy drinking.

1 cup flour

$^1/_2$ cup hazelnut flour

$^1/_3$ cup powdered sugar,
plus extra 1 tbsp, sifted

$^1/_2$ cup (1 stick) cold butter, chopped

1 egg yolk

1 tsp chilled water

$1^1/_2$ cups dessert wine

$^3/_4$ cup sugar

1 vanilla pod, split lengthwise

5 ripe plums, quartered, stones removed

2 cups mascarpone

$1^1/_4$ cups whipping cream

1 tbsp amaretto liqueur (see tips)

TIPS

- Instead of using amaretto liqueur, you can substitute 1 teaspoon of almond extract, if you like.
- If you put the pie dough in the freezer instead of the fridge, you can reduce the resting time by half.
- The pie crust can be made a day ahead. Store it in an airtight container.
- The poached plums in step 2 can be made several hours ahead of time. Refrigerate, still in the syrup, in an airtight container.

1   In a food processor, pulse the flour, hazelnut meal, and the $^1/_3$ cup of powdered sugar until just combined. Add the chilled butter; process again until the mixture resembles breadcrumbs. Combine the yolk and chilled water; add to the food processor and pulse until just combined. Form the dough into a disc, then wrap in plastic wrap. Refrigerate for 1 hour.

2   Meanwhile, stir the wine, sugar, and vanilla pod in a sauté pan over medium heat until the sugar dissolves. Bring to a boil. Add the plums. Simmer for 3 minutes or until just tender. Let the plums cool, still in the syrup, in the pan.

3   Roll out the pie dough between floured sheets of baking parchment until $^1/_8$in (4mm) thick and large enough to line a 9in (24cm) round fluted tart pan with a removable bottom. Place the pie dough into the pan, easing it into the bottom and side. Trim the edge. Cover. Refrigerate for 1 hour or until firm. (The pastry is quite delicate and may need to be chilled after rolling, before putting it in the tart pan.)

4   Preheat the oven to 400°F (200°C). Place the tart pan on a baking sheet. Line the dough with baking parchment; fill with dried beans or rice. Blind bake for 20 minutes. Carefully remove the parchment and beans. Bake for 10 minutes longer or until golden and cooked through. Let cool.

5   Meanwhile, strain the plums, reserving the syrup and vanilla pod. Peel the plums. Return the reserved syrup to the pan. Simmer for 20 minutes until reduced by half. Let cool. Return the plums to the syrup.

6   Put the mascarpone, whipping cream, liqueur, and the extra 1 tablespoon of sifted powdered sugar in a large bowl. Using a wooden spoon, fold the ingredients until combined. Cover with plastic wrap. Refrigerate.

7   Place the pie crust on a serving platter. Spoon the mascarpone mixture into the pie crust, then top with the poached plums and reserved vanilla pod. Drizzle with a little syrup. Serve immediately.

Apricot curd and verjus pavlovas

BAKED | PREP + COOK TIME **2 HOURS + COOLING + REFRIGERATION** | MAKES **6**

Verjus is a tangy condiment made from the pressed juice of unripe grapes. It adds a lovely acidity to sweet dishes. You'll find it sold in specialty stores and farmers markets, but if you can't locate some in either place, you can use apple cider vinegar instead.

3 eggs, room temperature

1½ cups sugar, divided

1 bunch of fresh rosemary

2 cups verjus

1 cup dried apricot halves

3 tbsp butter, room temperature

1 cup crème fraîche

1   Preheat the oven to 250°F (120°C). Line a large baking sheet with parchment paper.

2   Separate the eggs, putting the whites in the bowl of an electric mixer. Reserve the yolks. Using the electric mixer, beat the egg whites until soft peaks form. With the motor operating, gradually add ¾ cup of the sugar, beating until the sugar dissolves and the mixture is thick and glossy. Dollop 6 large spoonfuls of the meringue onto the lined baking sheet.

3   Bake the pavlovas for 1½ hours or until firm and dry. Turn off the oven and let the pavlovas cool in it with the door ajar.

4   Meanwhile, combine the remaining ¾ cup sugar, ⅔ cup water, 2 sprigs of rosemary, and the verjus in a medium saucepan over medium heat. Bring to a boil, stirring to dissolve the sugar. Cook for 2 minutes. Add the dried apricots; return to a boil. Cook for 3 minutes or until tender. Let cool. Reserve 1 cup of the poaching liquid.

5   To make the apricot curd, in a small saucepan, whisk together the reserved egg yolks and the reserved apricot poaching liquid. Cook, stirring continuously, over low heat for 4 minutes or until well thickened (do not allow to boil). Remove the pan from the heat. Whisk in the butter. Strain the curd into a small bowl. Cover the surface directly with plastic wrap. Refrigerate for 3 hours or until set.

6   Serve the pavlovas topped with the crème fraîche, apricot curd, and poached apricots in the remaining syrup.

TIPS

• Make the pavlovas and the poached apricots up to a day ahead. Store the pavlovas in an airtight container at room temperature, and the apricots in the fridge.

• For a flavorful alternative, add ½ teaspoon ground cardamom to the whipped egg whites with the sugar in step 2. Alternatively, add strips of orange zest to the syrup in step 4.

• To make a festive garnish from the remaining rosemary sprigs, brush them with an extra egg white, then sprinkle with 1 tablespoon sugar. Place on a separate baking sheet, and bake for 1 hour alongside the pavlovas until dried.

Fig and vincotto bread pudding

BAKED | PREP + COOK TIME **1 HOUR 20 MINUTES + STANDING** | SERVES **6**

Vincotto, or vino cotto, is a type of fermented grape juice from Italy which has a sweet acidity perfect for both sweet and savory foods. If you can't find vincotto at a specialty market, you can use a balsamic glaze or reduced balsamic vinegar instead.

7 tbsp butter

1lb (450g) sourdough fruit and walnut loaf

6 eggs

1/2 cup sugar

4 cups milk

1lb (450g) large, fresh figs (see tips)

1/2 cup vincotto (see tips)

1 Using some of the butter, grease a 9in (23cm) round, 2½in (6cm) deep 8-cup (2l) ovenproof dish.

2 Remove the crusts from the bread. Cut the bread into 2in (5mm) thick slices. Spread the slices with the remaining butter. Arrange the bread slices in a circular pattern in the dish. Whisk together the eggs, sugar, and milk in a large bowl until combined. Pour over the bread. Let stand for 30 minutes for the bread to soften.

3 Meanwhile, preheat the oven to 350°F (180°C).

4 Place the baking dish in a large roasting pan. Add enough boiling water to the pan to come halfway up the side of the dish. Gently transfer the pan to the oven. Bake the bread pudding for 50 minutes or until just set.

5 Cut the figs into slices or wedges. Serve the pudding topped with the figs and drizzled with the vincotto.

TIPS

- You can use green or black figs, but for the best flavor they must be ripe.
- Vincotto is Italian for "cooked wine." Traditionally it is made by boiling down grape must—the juice and pulp of wine-making grapes—to make a thick, versatile syrupy condiment. Look for it online or at an Italian specialty market.
- If you want something a little out of the ordinary, in step 2 add 1 teaspoon ground cinnamon to the butter before spreading it on the bread.

Black Forest soufflé

BAKED | PREP + COOK TIME **55 MINUTES** | SERVES **4**

Two classic desserts combine scrumptiously and effortlessly in this easy recipe, where a light-as-air French soufflé meets the kirsch-spiked cherry and chocolate flavors of Germany's Black Forest cake.

4 tbsp butter

$1/3$ cup sugar, plus ¼ cup extra to coat the dishes

10.5oz (300g) dark chocolate (at least 70% cocoa)

6 eggs, room temperature, separated

3 egg whites, room temperature

2 tsp powdered sugar

whipped cream, for serving

poached cherries

1 x 15oz (425g) can seedless black cherries in syrup

$1/4$ cup sugar

2in (5cm) strip of orange zest

2 tbsp kirsch or cherry brandy

1   To make the poached cherries, drain the cherries over a bowl. Reserve the syrup. Set the cherries aside. Stir together the syrup, sugar, and orange zest in a medium saucepan. Next, stir over high heat, without boiling, until the sugar dissolves. Bring to a boil. Reduce the heat. Simmer, uncovered, for about 5 minutes or until the syrup thickens slightly. Remove from the heat. Stir in the cherries and kirsch.

2   Preheat the oven to 400°F (200°C). Butter four $1^1/4$-cup ovenproof soufflé dishes; sprinkle them evenly with the $1/4$ cup of sugar. Shake out any excess sugar.

3   Break the chocolate into a large heatproof bowl over a large saucepan of simmering water (don't let the water touch the base of the bowl). Stir until the chocolate is melted. Let cool for 5 minutes. Stir in the egg yolks until smooth and combined.

4   Using an electric mixer, beat all 9 egg whites and the $1/3$ cup of sugar in a medium bowl until stiff peaks form. Working in 2 batches, gently fold into the chocolate mixture. Divide the mixture among the prepared soufflé dishes. Smooth the tops. Carefully place the dishes on a baking sheet. Bake the soufflés for about 15 minutes until puffed and risen.

5   Dust the soufflés with the sifted powdered sugar. Serve immediately with the poached cherries and a dollop of whipped cream.

TIP

Serve with vanilla bean ice cream instead of the whipped cream or, for a real treat, use both!

Lemon passion fruit creams with shortbread

BAKED AND SET | PREP + COOK TIME **45 MINUTES + OVERNIGHT REFRIGERATION** | SERVES **6**

Buttery shortbread provides a foil for these unctuous custard desserts. While fresh
passion fruit pulp is best for this recipe, if you can't find it you can use canned pulp instead.
Just make sure it doesn't have any added sugar in it.

You will need to start this recipe a day ahead

2½ cups whipping cream

¼ cup sugar

2 tsp grated lemon zest

¼ cup lemon juice

⅓ cup passion fruit pulp

5oz (150g) fresh blueberries, to garnish

lemon shortbread cookies

¾ cup cold butter

⅓ cup sugar

1¾ cups flour

½ tsp salt

1 tsp lemon zest

1   Put the cream and sugar in a heavy-based saucepan over high heat. Stir continuously until the mixture boils. Reduce the heat to medium. Simmer, stirring, for 2 minutes longer. Remove from the heat. Let cool for 10 minutes.

2   Add the lemon juice and zest to the cream mixture. Stir gently for 5 seconds. Do not overmix. Pour into six ¾-cup glasses or small, wide bowls. Spoon half of the passion fruit pulp into the lemon mixture. Refrigerate overnight until set.

3   To make the lemon shortbread cookies, chop the cold butter. In a food processor, pulse the chopped butter, sugar, flour, salt, and lemon zest until combined. With the motor operating, add 1 tablespoon cold water. Process until the mixture forms a soft ball. Divide the dough in half. Flatten each portion into a disc. Wrap each one in plastic wrap. Refrigerate for 20 minutes or until firm.

4   Preheat the oven to 350°F (180°C).

5   Roll out each disc of shortbread dough between lightly floured sheets of parchment paper until ⅛in (3mm) thick. Remove the top sheet of baking parchment; transfer the dough on the paper to the baking sheets. Bake for 15 minutes or until the shortbread is golden. Cut into shards while still warm. Let cool on the baking sheets.

6   Top the lemon passion fruit creams with the remaining passion fruit and the blueberries. Serve with the lemon shortbread cookies.

TIPS

• The citric acid in the lemon reacts with the cream to thicken it.

• Instead of blueberries, top with sliced strawberries or raspberries, if you like.

• The shortbread can be stored in an airtight container for up to 1 week.

Frozen raspberry, yogurt, and strawberry terrine

FROZEN | PREP + COOK TIME 1 HOUR + FREEZING, REFRIGERATION + STANDING | SERVES 10

When it comes to terrines, most people think of savory versions, but dessert terrines can be a stunning end to a meal and a lighter option, especially when summer fruit is at its best. This celebration of berries is sure to become a favorite summer make-ahead treat.

8oz (225g) raspberries
8oz (225g) strawberries, hulled, quartered
1/4 cup sugar
1/3 cup firmly packed small mint leaves

raspberry sorbet
8oz (225g) frozen raspberries
1/4 cup boiling water
1 tbsp corn syrup
2 tbsp powdered sugar

yogurt sorbet
1/2 cup milk
1/4 cup sugar
1 tbsp corn syrup
3/4 cup Greek yogurt

strawberry sorbet
8oz (225g) strawberries, halved
1/4 cup boiling water
1 tbsp corn syrup
1/4 cup powdered sugar

1 Line the bottom and sides of a 4-cup loaf pan with plastic wrap. Freeze until needed.

2 To make the raspberry sorbet, in a food processor, pulse the raspberries until coarsely crushed. Combine the water and corn syrup in a liquid measuring cup. Gradually add to the processor while the motor is operating. Process for 3 minutes or until smooth. Add the powdered sugar. Process until combined. Spoon the mixture into the prepared loaf pan. Smooth the surface. Cover with plastic wrap. Freeze for 2 hours or until the raspberry sorbet is firm.

3 To make the yogurt sorbet, stir the milk, sugar, and corn syrup in a small saucepan until the sugar is dissolved. Bring to a boil. Remove from the heat. Let cool, then whisk in the yogurt. Refrigerate until cold. Remove the plastic wrap from the raspberry sorbet. Spoon the cold yogurt sorbet over it. Smooth the surface. Cover with plastic wrap. Freeze for 4 hours or until firm.

4 To make the strawberry sorbet, in a food processor, pulse the strawberries until coarsely chopped. Combine the water and corn syrup in a liquid measuring cup. Gradually add to the processor while the motor is operating. Process for 3 minutes or until smooth. Add the powdered sugar. Process until combined. Refrigerate until cold. Remove the plastic wrap from the loaf pan. Spoon the cold strawberry sorbet over the yogurt sorbet. Smooth the surface. Cover with plastic wrap. Freeze overnight.

5 Combine the raspberries, strawberries, sugar, and half of the mint leaves in a medium bowl. Let stand at room temperature for 20 minutes, stirring occasionally, or until the sugar is dissolved.

6 Dip the pan briefly in hot water, then turn the dessert out of the pan. Serve topped with the berry mixture and remaining mint leaves.

Cookie dough and blackberry ice cream loaf

FROZEN | PREP + COOK TIME **15 MINUTES + FREEZING + STANDING** | SERVES **8**

The longest part about making this dessert is the freezing time, yet it looks as if you have slaved over it for hours. To make a bespoke dessert, use your favorite ice cream flavor. Chocolate and caramel-flavored ice cream would work very well in this recipe.

4 cups vanilla bean ice cream

$2/3$ cup roasted salted macadamia nuts, plus extra, for serving (optional)

7oz (200g) purchased edible chocolate chip cookie dough (see tips)

$1/2$ cup purchased chocolate topping, divided, plus extra, for serving (optional)

$1/2$ cup fresh or frozen blackberries, plus extra, for serving (optional)

TIPS

- It is not advisable to eat homemade raw cookie dough. Purpose-made frozen edible cookie dough uses pasteurized eggs and heat-treated flour, to ensure food safety. If you cannot find it, simply use cookie dough ice cream instead, halving the amount of vanilla bean ice cream and using it only for the blackberry half of the ice cream loaf.
- If you don't have a loaf pan exactly the dimensions specified in the recipe that is fine, as long as the cup capacity is similar. To check the cup capacity of your dish, fill it to the rim with cup measures of water, keeping track of how much you add.
- You can make the ice cream loaf up to 3 days ahead of time. Cover and freeze until needed.
- Use other frozen berries, such as raspberries or strawberries, instead of the blackberries, or when fresh berries are not in season.

1 Scoop half of the ice cream into a medium bowl (return the remaining half to the freezer until needed). Let stand for 15 minutes or until softened slightly.

2 Grease a 5¼in x 9½in (13.5cm x 24cm)/9-cup loaf pan. Line the bottom and long sides with parchment paper, extending the paper 1in (2.5cm) over the sides. Sprinkle the macadamia nuts over the bottom of the pan.

3 Chop the cookie dough into ½in (1cm) pieces. Add the cookie dough to the softened ice cream with ¼ cup of the chocolate topping. Mix until smooth. Spread the ice cream mixture over the macadamia nuts. Spread the remaining chocolate topping over the ice cream mixture. Freeze for 1 hour or until firm.

4 After 45 minutes, remove the remaining vanilla ice cream from the freezer. Scoop into a medium bowl to soften. Mix in the blackberries. Spread the blackberry ice cream mixture over the cookie dough ice cream in the loaf pan. Freeze for 4 hours or overnight until firm.

5 Remove the ice cream loaf from the freezer 10 minutes before serving, to let it soften slightly. Serve in thick slices with extra macadamia nuts, blackberries, and chocolate topping, if you like.

Mango cheesecake tart

BAKED AND FRESH | PREP + COOK TIME **1 HOUR 5 MINUTES + REFRIGERATION** | SERVES **6**

The shape and size of this crowd-pleasing dessert make it easy to cut and serve to a larger gathering of people, and its straightforward final assembly means that you won't be stuck in the kitchen, left out of the party, while all your guests are enjoying themselves.

1¹/₂ cups flour

2 tbsp sugar, plus extra ¼ cup

5 tbsp butter

16oz (453g) (2 packages) cream cheese, softened, divided

1 tsp vanilla extract

¼ cup fresh coconut flakes

¹/₃ cup milk

2 mangoes (see tips)

1 To make the pie crusts, process the flour, the 2 tablespoons sugar, butter, and 4oz (125g) of the cream cheese until a dough starts to form. Knead the dough on a lightly floured work surface until just combined. Wrap in plastic wrap. Refrigerate for 30 minutes.

2 Roll the dough between 2 lightly floured sheets of parchment paper until large enough to line a 4in x 14in (11cm x 35cm) rectangular tart pan with a removable bottom. Lift the pie dough into the pan, easing it into the bottom and sides. Trim the edges. Prick the bottom of the pie dough with a fork. Refrigerate for 10 minutes.

3 Meanwhile, put the coconut flakes on a baking sheet. Place in the cold oven, then turn it on to 350°F (180°C) to preheat for the tart. Roast the coconut for 6 minutes or until lightly golden. Set aside.

4 Line the dough with parchment paper cut to fit. Fill with dried beans or rice. Blind bake for 15 minutes. Remove the parchment and beans. Bake for 20 minutes longer or until the pie crust is golden. Let cool.

5 Meanwhile, combine the milk, the extra ¹/₄ cup sugar, the remaining cream cheese, and the vanilla until smooth. Spoon the mixture into the cooled pie crust, spreading evenly over the bottom.

6 Cut cheeks from the mangoes. Hold the mango cheek in your hand, skin side down, and use a metal spoon to scoop the flesh out of the skin in one piece. Slice the peeled fruit into thin slices. Repeat with each mango cheek. Arrange the slices on top of the tart.

TIPS

• Instead of mango, you can use pineapple or star fruit for an equally tropical feel.
• Cut the flesh from around the mango stone and freeze for use in smoothies later.

Mixed berry clafoutis

BAKED | PREP + COOK TIME **45 MINUTES** | SERVES **4**

The classic dessert clafoutis, from the Limousin region of France, traditionally consists of black cherries baked in a sweet, custard-like batter. Here, we've swapped the cherries for mixed berries, such as strawberries and blackberries, for a flavorful twist.

a little softened butter, for greasing

$^2/_3$ cup milk

$^2/_3$ cup whipping cream

1 cinnamon stick

1 tsp vanilla extract

4 eggs

$^1/_2$ cup sugar

$^1/_4$ cup flour

2 cups frozen mixed berries

powdered sugar, sifted, for dusting

vanilla ice cream or whipped cream, for serving (optional)

1   Preheat the oven to 400°F (200°C). Butter a 6-cup oven safe dish or skillet.

2   Put the milk, whipping cream, cinnamon, and vanilla extract in a medium saucepan. Bring to a boil, then immediately remove from the heat. Discard the cinnamon stick.

3   Whisk together the eggs and sugar in a medium bowl until light and frothy. Whisk in the flour, then gradually whisk in the milk-cream mixture.

4   Sprinkle the berries over the bottom of the prepared dish. Pour the batter over the berries. Bake for 35 minutes or until browned lightly and set. Serve the clafoutis warm, dusted with sifted powdered sugar and topped with a scoop of ice cream or whipped cream, if you like.

Elderflower, vodka, and cranberry ice pops

FROZEN | PREP + COOK TIME **25 MINUTES + FREEZING** | MAKES **24**

These ice pops for adults are wonderful to serve at parties and gatherings during the long days of summer. Tart and fresh, with floral and minty undertones, these treats, once served, will not last long enough to even begin to melt.

⅓ cup vodka

½ cup elderflower cordial

2 tbsp strained lime juice

1 cup sparkling mineral water

2 tbsp thinly sliced mint leaves

3 cups cranberry juice

1 Combine the vodka, elderflower cordial, lime juice, and mineral water in a large pitcher. Divide the mixture evenly among the ice pop molds (see tips), filling each mold about halfway full. Sprinkle evenly with the mint. Insert the sticks. Freeze for 6 hours or until the mixture is frozen.

2 Pour the cranberry juice over the vodka mint layer. Freeze for 2 hours or until the juice is frozen.

3 Just before serving, rub the outside of the molds with a hot kitchen towel to loosen. Gently remove the ice pops, and serve immediately.

TIPS

• You will need 12 to 24 ice pop molds, depending on their size, and sticks for freezing.

• Instead of ice pop molds, you can use small plastic cups or shot glasses. After filling, cover each one with a piece of plastic wrap and insert the stick through a hole pierced in the plastic wrap. (The plastic wrap will help to keep the sticks upright while the ice pops set.)

• The ice pops can be made several days ahead.

CHOCOLATE AND COFFEE

Rich mousses, spectacular tarts and pastries,
puddings and soufflés oozy with goodness—
this is the chapter for those who consider
chocolate and coffee flavor imperatives.

Coffee chocolate crunch wreath

FROZEN | PREP + COOK TIME **45 MINUTES + FREEZING** | SERVES **12**

Creating this frozen dessert in the form of a wreath gives it a celebratory feel—and makes
it easy to serve sliced so everyone gets to enjoy a little of the goodies sprinkled on top.
The coffee-macadamia ice cream sits on a crunchy cookie base, adding to the enticement.

You will need to start this recipe a day ahead

butter for greasing

1 tbsp instant espresso powder

1¹/₂ tbsp coffee liqueur

2¹/₂ cups whipping cream

2¹/₂ cups powdered sugar, sifted

1lb (450g) mascarpone

¹/₄ cup chocolate-coated coffee beans, chopped, plus extra, to garnish

1 cup coarsely chopped honey-roasted macadamia nuts, divided (see tips)

30 premade chocolates, such as truffles, to garnish (see tips)

cocoa powder, sifted, to dust (optional)

crunchy cookie base

8oz (225g) crunchy chocolate chip cookies

1 cup chocolate-coated malt balls

4 tbsp butter, melted

TIPS

- Choose a mix of chocolates, in varying sizes and shapes, for the best visual effect.
- You can use any honey-roasted or candied nuts, including cashews and pecans.
- The wreath can be made up to 3 days ahead.

1 Grease a 9in (24cm) springform pan. Line the bottom with parchment paper. Wrap a 3¹/₂in (9cm) ramekin (or other straight-sided round dish) with a double layer of plastic wrap. Grease the plastic. Place the ramekin in the center of the pan.

2 Combine the espresso powder and ¹/₄ cup boiling water in a small bowl. Stir to dissolve, then stir in the liqueur. Let cool.

3 Using an electric mixer, beat together the cream and powdered sugar in a large bowl until soft peaks form. Fold in the mascarpone, the chocolate-coated coffee beans, and ³/₄ cup of the macadamia nuts, then fold in the coffee mixture until just combined.

4 Spoon the mixture into the prepared pan. Smooth the top. Freeze for 4 hours or until firm.

5 Meanwhile, to make the crunchy cookie base, add the chocolate chip cookies and malted milk balls to the bowl of a food processor. Pulse into coarse crumbs. Add the melted butter. Process briefly to combine.

6 Press the cookie mixture over the top of the ice cream to form a smooth surface. Cover with plastic wrap. Freeze overnight.

7 To serve, run a knife around the edge of the ramekin to release it. Remove it from the middle of the pan. Working quickly, run a knife around the outside of the wreath. If needed, rub the outside of the pan with a hot, damp cloth to loosen. Place an inverted serving plate on top of the pan and carefully turn over. Remove the collar, the bottom of the pan (now the top of your wreath), and the parchment paper. Top the wreath with the remaining macadamia nuts, chocolates, and extra chocolate-coated coffee beans. Dust with a little sifted cocoa powder, if you like.

Figgy brownies with chocolate caramel sauce

BAKED | PREP + COOK TIME **45 MINUTES** | MAKES **9**

Ice cream performs double duty in this recipe, acting as a unique trick to create a decadent dessert sauce as well as an accompaniment to the brownies. Soft, moist figs add a rich sweetness to the brownies, completing the symphony of culinary gratification.

8oz (225g) soft dried figs (see tips)

12oz (340g) dark chocolate chips, divided

½ cup butter, plus extra for greasing

³/₄ cup sugar

3 eggs

³/₄ cup flour

½ tsp baking soda

1 tsp baking powder

1 tsp salt

2 pints (1l) salted caramel ice cream, divided

grated chocolate, for serving

1 Preheat the oven to 350°F (180°C). Grease a 9in x 9in (20cm x 20cm) baking dish. Line the bottom with parchment paper.

2 Remove and discard the hard tops from the figs. Coarsely chop the figs. Cut the butter into cubes.

3 Place 1¼ cups of the chocolate chips, the butter, and sugar in a large heatproof bowl over a large saucepan of simmering water (don't let the bowl touch the water). Stir until melted. Let cool. Reserve the pan of water.

4 Whisk the eggs into the chocolate mixture until combined. Fold in the flour, baking soda, baking powder, and salt until just combined. Fold in the figs until just combined. Pour the brownie mixture into the prepared baking dish.

5 Bake for 25–30 minutes or until a wooden skewer inserted into the center comes out with moist crumbs attached. Leave in the dish for 5 minutes.

6 Meanwhile, to make the chocolate caramel sauce, reheat the reserved pan of water over medium-low heat until simmering. Place the remaining chocolate in a large heatproof bowl with 1 cup of the ice cream. Place the bowl over the pan of simmering water, then stir until melted and smooth. Remove the bowl from the pan.

7 Cut the brownie into 9 squares. Serve drizzled with the chocolate caramel sauce and sprinkled with the grated chocolate, accompanied by the remaining ice cream.

TIPS

- Soft, juicy figs are simply dried figs that are not as hard as traditional dried figs.
- Serve the brownies topped with toasted walnuts, almonds, or hazelnuts, if you like.
- Use high-quality vanilla or chocolate ice cream instead of salted caramel ice cream.

Cherry and orange chocolate puff

BAKED | PREP + COOK TIME **35 MINUTES + STANDING** | SERVES **6**

No one ever needs to know how simple it is to make this rich pastry. Using premade puff pastry and good quality chocolate creates a delicious pastry worth of a bakery. Chocolate and cherries are, it goes without saying, a divine combination.

2 sheets of frozen puff pastry, just thawed

2 x 3.5oz (100g) bars of white chocolate

3.5oz (100g) bar of orange-flavored dark chocolate (at least 70% cocoa) (see tips)

2 tbsp dried tart cherries (see tips)

1 egg, lightly beaten

2 tbsp natural flaked almonds

2 tsp powdered sugar, sifted

vanilla ice cream, for serving

1 Preheat the oven to 375°F (190°C). Line a large baking sheet with parchment paper.

2 Place 1 sheet of the puff pastry on the lined baking sheet. Stack the white chocolate bars in the center of the pastry. Top with the dark chocolate bar. Surround the stacked chocolate with the dried cherries.

3 Lightly brush the edges of the pastry with the beaten egg. Place the remaining pastry sheet over the top to cover the base.

4 Gently fold the edges in a pleated pattern, from the outside inward, around the chocolate and cherries. Tuck the ends upward to seal. Lightly brush the pastry with more of the beaten egg. Scatter the almonds over the top.

5 Bake for 25 minutes or until the pastry is cooked through and golden. Let stand on the baking sheet for 15 minutes.

6 Dust the puff with the sifted powdered sugar. Serve sliced, accompanied by the vanilla ice cream.

TIPS

- You can find chocolate bars in all kinds of fruit flavors. Try raspberry for a nice substitute.
- Swap the dried cherries for dried cranberries, raisins, or golden raisins, if you like.
- The puff can be made a day ahead to the end of step 4. Bake just before serving.

Chocolate tartlets with berries

BAKED | PREP + COOK TIME **40 MINUTES + COOLING** | MAKES **6**

Rich chocolate and tart–sweet berries are a match made in heaven. Using puff pastry instead of a traditional pie crust for these tartlets is not only quicker, but it lightens this decadent flavor pairing as well.

butter for greasing

3 egg yolks

$1/2$ cup sugar

2 tbsp cornstarch

$1/4$ tsp salt

1 tbsp cocoa powder

$3/4$ cup milk

$2/3$ cup whipping cream

1 sheet of puff pastry, just thawed

5oz (150g) fresh raspberries

5oz (150g) fresh blueberries

1 tbsp powdered sugar, sifted

1 Preheat the oven to 425°F (220°C). Grease 6 holes of a regular size ($1/3$ cup) 12-hole muffin pan.

2 To make the chocolate custard filling, combine the egg yolks, sugar, cornstarch, cocoa powder, and salt in a medium saucepan. Whisk in the milk and cream until smooth. Stir over medium heat until the mixture boils and thickens. (It will thicken quickly.) Transfer to a heatproof bowl; strain if needed. Cover the surface with plastic wrap. Let cool.

3 Meanwhile, cut the pastry sheet in half. Stack the 2 halves; press firmly. Roll up the pastry tightly from the short side. Cut the log into 6 slices. Place the slices between sheets of baking parchment, then roll them to form 4in (12cm) rounds. Press the rounds into the holes of the prepared muffin pan.

4 Spoon the chocolate custard into the pastry shells. Bake for about 20 minutes or until set. Let cool in the pan.

5 Serve the tarts topped with the raspberries and blueberries, then dusted with the sifted powdered sugar.

Profiteroles

BAKED | PREP + COOK TIME **1 HOUR 10 MINUTES + COOLING** | MAKES **16**

The choux pastries become profiteroles when they're filled, but they're not your commonplace profiteroles filled with whipped cream and topped with chocolate sauce. Instead, they're filled with a scoop of ice cream and dusted with a little powdered sugar.

³/₄ cup water

4 tbsp butter, chopped

1 tsp sugar

³/₄ cup flour

3 eggs

1 pint (473ml) vanilla ice cream, softened slightly

powdered sugar, sifted, to dust

1 Preheat the oven to 400°F (200°C). Line two baking sheets with parchment paper.

2 Combine the water, butter, and sugar in a medium saucepan over low heat until the butter has melted. Bring to a boil. Add the flour. Beat with a wooden spoon for 2 minutes or until the mixture comes away from the bottom of the pan and forms a ball.

3 Transfer the pastry to the small bowl of an electric mixer. Let cool, then beat in the eggs one at a time, beating well after each addition, until it comes together to form a consistent, sticky pastry dough.

4 Drop 16 level tablespoons of the dough onto the prepared baking sheets, placing them 2in (5cm) apart. Bake for 20 minutes. Reduce the oven temperature to 350°F (180°C). Bake for 10 minutes longer or until golden and firm. Turn off the oven, and allow the choux to cool in the oven with the door ajar.

5 Using a sharp knife, split the choux in half. Fill each one with a small scoop of ice cream. Dust the profiteroles with a little powdered sugar.

TIP

Use your favorite flavor of ice cream such as chocolate or salted caramel instead of vanilla. Or try the coffee and caramel variation on page 64. You will find a cream-filled option topped with chocolate there, too.

Profiterole variations

You don't need to be daunted at the idea of making your own profiteroles. Tackling choux pastry is not difficult as long as you follow the instructions to the letter. You can then fill the pastries with fillings using any of the combinations below.

Cream filling and chocolate sauce

Make the profiteroles as described through step 4 on page 62. To make the chocolate sauce, chop 3.5oz (100g) each of dark and milk chocolate. Place in a small saucepan with $1/2$ cup heavy cream. Stir over low heat until just smooth. For the filling, whisk 1 cup mascarpone, 1 cup heavy cream, 1 teaspoon vanilla extract, and 2 teaspoons powdered sugar to soft peaks. Fill the split profiteroles with the mascarpone cream. Drizzle with the chocolate sauce.

Crushed berries and cream

Make the profiteroles as described through step 4 on page 62. Combine 5oz (150g) raspberries and 2 tablespoons powdered sugar in a bowl. Mash with a fork until soft. Add 1 pint (473ml) softened vanilla ice cream. Fold together. Fill each of the split profiteroles with a scoop of the raspberry ice cream. Freeze. Stir $1/2$ cup berry jam and $1/2$ cup pomegranate juice in a saucepan over medium heat for 3 minutes or until thickened. Serve the profiteroles drizzled with the syrup.

Custard and caramel

Make the profiteroles as described through step 4 on page 62. Beat 1 cup mascarpone with $1/2$ cup premade or instant vanilla pudding until thick. Fill the split profiteroles with the custard. Place on a parchment-lined baking sheet. Stir 1 cup sugar, 1 tsp salt, and $1/2$ cup of water in a saucepan over medium heat, without boiling, until dissolved. Boil without stirring until golden. Drizzle the profiteroles with the caramel. (Take care, as it will be very hot.)

Coffee ice cream and caramel

Make the profiteroles as described on page 62, using coffee or caramel ice cream instead of vanilla, and folding in $1^1/2$ cups chopped honey-roasted or candied nuts. Freeze. Stir a 13.4oz (380g) can of dulce de leche in a small saucepan over medium heat with 2 tablespoons each of rum and water until smooth and of a drizzling consistency. Serve the profiteroles drizzled with the warm rum-caramel sauce.

Chocolate soufflé with chocolate and sherry sauce

BAKED | PREP + COOK TIME **45 MINUTES + COOLING** | MAKES **8**

The best sweet sherry to use in this recipe is Pedro Ximénez. A dark, syrupy style of sherry, it has a wonderful affinity with chocolate. Whichever particular sherry you choose, it should always be good quality and something that you would happily drink.

4 tbsp butter, softened

1/3 cup sugar, divided

6 eggs

1 1/4 cups milk, divided

10oz (275g) dark chocolate chips, divided

1 tbsp cornstarch

1/2 tsp salt

1/4 cup sweet sherry, such as Pedro Ximénez (see tips)

TIPS

- You may use coffee- or orange-flavored liqueur instead of the sherry.
- Keep the unused egg yolks, covered, in the fridge to make your own mayonnaise, lemon butter, or hollandaise sauce.
- Serve with scoops of vanilla bean ice cream.
- You could also serve a small glass of sherry with the soufflés, if you like.

1 Preheat the oven to 375°F (190°C). Grease eight 1/2-cup (125ml) ramekins or heatproof dishes with soft butter. Coat the bottoms and sides with 2 tablespoons of the sugar, then shake out any excess. Place the ramekins on a baking sheet.

2 Separate the eggs: place 6 egg whites in the bowl of an electric mixer and 3 egg yolks in a medium bowl. Keep the remaining egg yolks for another use (see tips).

3 Put 1 cup of the milk in a medium saucepan over medium heat. Add 3.5 ounces (100g) of the chocolate to the pan. Stir with a whisk until the chocolate melts and the mixture is smooth and almost boiling.

4 Add the cornstarch, remaining sugar, and salt to the egg yolks. Whisk until smooth. Whisk 1/4 cup of the hot chocolate mixture into the egg yolk mixture until combined. Pour the mixture back into the saucepan. Whisk continuously over medium heat until the mixture boils and thickens. Transfer to a large bowl. Cover the surface directly with plastic wrap. Let cool for 15 minutes.

5 Using an electric mixer, beat the egg whites until stiff peaks form. With a large metal spoon, stir one-third of the egg whites through the warm chocolate mixture. Fold in the remaining egg whites until just combined.

6 Spoon the soufflé mixture into the prepared ramekins. Smooth the surface level with the top of the dish. Bake for 12 minutes or until the soufflés are puffed.

7 Meanwhile, to make the chocolate sauce, put the remaining chocolate in a small heavy-based saucepan. Add the remaining milk and the sherry. Stir over medium heat until smooth.

8 Serve the soufflés immediately, drizzled with the hot chocolate sauce.

Chocolate mousse shots

SET | PREP + COOK TIME **25 MINUTES + REFRIGERATION** | SERVES **4**

These chocolate "shots" are perfect for when you're craving a little something sweet, and the small serving size prevents you from going overboard. The tart raspberries cut through the sweetness of the mousse beautifully. This dessert proves that less is more.

1³/₄ oz (50g) dark chocolate (at least 70% cocoa), finely chopped

¹/₂ cup fresh soft ricotta cheese, room temperature

¹/₄ cup sugar

3 tsp Dutch-process cocoa powder (see tips)

¹/₄ tsp salt

2 egg whites

1 cup fresh raspberries, to garnish

1 Stir the chocolate in a medium heatproof bowl over a medium saucepan of simmering water (don't let the water touch the base of the bowl) until melted. Let cool for 10 minutes.

2 Meanwhile, in a large bowl, stir together the ricotta cheese, sugar, cocoa powder, and salt until smooth. Add the melted chocolate. Mix until combined.

3 Using an electric mixer, beat the egg whites in a small bowl until soft peaks form. Fold the egg whites into the chocolate mixture in 2 batches. Pour the mixture into four ¹/₂-cup glasses. Cover and refrigerate for 6 hours or until the mousse is firm.

4 Serve the mousse topped with the raspberries.

TIPS

- If the ricotta is too cold and the melted chocolate becomes too firm, simply microwave for 15 seconds to soften before folding in the egg whites.
- Dutch-process cocoa powder is darker than natural cocoa powder and has a mellower flavor. It goes through an alkalizing process when it is made, neutralizing the natural acidity of the cocoa beans.
- The mousse will keep, in the refrigerator, for up to 3 days.

White chocolate and caramel ripple mousse

SET | PREP + COOK TIME **20 MINUTES + REFRIGERATION** | SERVES **6**

With just a few ingredients and a small investment of time, you will create an irresistibly smooth white chocolate mousse that is lifted out of the ordinary by a swirl of delicious caramel. Tart raspberries cap it all off.

1¼ cups white chocolate baking chips

³/₄ cup whipping cream

3 egg whites

¹/₂ cup canned dulce de leche

¹/₂ cup premade thick chocolate sauce

125g fresh raspberries

1 Put the white chocolate baking chips and whipping cream in a small heatproof bowl over a small saucepan of gently simmering water (don't allow the bowl to touch the water). Stir until melted and smooth. Remove the bowl from the pan. Refrigerate for 30 minutes or until chilled and slightly thickened.

2 Using an electric mixer, beat the egg whites in a medium bowl until almost stiff peaks form. Fold into the cooled chocolate mixture.

3 In a small bowl, combine the dulce de leche and chocolate sauce. Add all but a few tablespoons of the chocolate caramel mixture to the white chocolate and gently swirl through. Place the remaining chocolate-caramel sauce in the bottom of six ³/₄-cup glasses. Spoon the mousse over the sauce in each glass. Refrigerate for 5 hours or until just set.

4 Serve the mousse topped with the raspberries.

TIPS

- Top the mousse with sliced fresh figs instead of raspberries, if you like.
- The mousse can be made up to a day ahead.

Chocolate sesame tarts

SET | PREP + COOK TIME **30 MINUTES + REFRIGERATION** | MAKES **6**

Finishing these tarts with a sprinkling of sesame seeds adds a wonderful toasty flavor and elevates this quick and easy chocolate dessert into something special. The sesame seeds add a signature aroma. With the orange zest, they ensure these treats smell as good as they look.

7 tbsp butter

7oz (200g) crispy butter cookies

1 small orange

7oz (200g) dark chocolate (70% cocoa), broken into pieces

$1^1/_4$ cup whipping cream, divided

2 tbsp sugar

$^1/_2$ tsp salt

1 tsp black sesame seeds, toasted, to garnish (see tips)

1. Melt the butter in a small saucepan or in a small heatproof bowl in the microwave. Pulse the cookies in the food processor until they form fine crumbs. In a large bowl, combine the crumbs and melted butter. Divide the cookie mixture among six $^3/_4$in (2cm) deep, $3^1/_4$in (8.5cm) (base measure) round fluted tart pans with removable bottoms. Press the mixture evenly over the bases and sides. Refrigerate for 30 minutes or until firm.

2. Meanwhile, finely grate the zest from the orange; you will need 2 teaspoons. Juice half the orange; you will need $^1/_4$ cup of orange juice.

3. Put the chocolate, $^3/_4$ cup of the whipping cream, the sugar, and the salt in a small saucepan. Stir over low heat until melted and combined. Stir in the orange juice and 1 teaspoon of the zest. Pour the mixture into the tart shells. Refrigerate for 4 hours or until set.

4. Using an electric mixer, beat the remaining whipping cream in a small bowl until soft peaks form.

5. Serve the tarts sprinkled with the sesame seeds and orange zest, topped with a dollop of the whipped cream.

TIPS

- You can use white sesame seeds instead of black sesame seeds, if you prefer.
- Serve the tarts with coconut gelato, if you like.

Churros with chili chocolate

FRIED | PREP + COOK TIME **40 MINUTES** | SERVES **6**

The flavor pairing of chocolate and chili might seem unexpected, but it actually works to awaken all your taste buds. The chocolate dipping sauce here is zingy and rich, and a mouth-watering foil to the crisp churros. True indulgence doesn't get much better than this.

7 tbsp butter, coarsely chopped

1 cup flour, sifted

3 eggs

vegetable oil for deep-frying

$^1\!/_3$ cup sugar

1 tsp ground cinnamon

chili chocolate sauce

3.5oz (100g) dark chocolate (at least 70% cocoa), broken into pieces

2 tbsp butter

$^3\!/_4$ cup whipping cream

pinch of chili powder

1 To make the chili chocolate sauce, break the chocolate into pieces into a medium heatproof bowl. Add the butter, cream, and chili powder. Stir over a medium saucepan of simmering water (do not allow the water to touch the bottom of the bowl) until smooth. Set aside to keep warm.

2 Bring the butter and 1 cup water to a boil in a medium saucepan. Add the sifted flour. Beat with a wooden spoon over medium heat until the mixture comes away from the bottom and side of the pan and forms a smooth ball.

3 Transfer the mixture to a small bowl. Using an electric mixer, beat in the eggs, one at a time, on medium speed for about 1 minute or until the mixture becomes glossy. Let cool for 10 minutes.

4 Meanwhile, fill a large, wide saucepan two-thirds full of vegetable oil; be careful not to overfill. Heat to 375°F (190°C) (or until the oil sizzles when a small cube of bread is added). Spoon the mixture into a piping bag fitted with a ½in (1cm) fluted tube. Squeeze 6in (15cm) lengths of dough into the hot oil, cutting off the lengths with a sharp knife or scissors. Deep-fry about 4 strips at a time for about 2 minutes on each side or until lightly browned and crisp. Drain the churros on paper towels. Toss the hot churros in the combined sugar and cinnamon.

5 Serve immediately with small bowls or large cups of the warm chili chocolate sauce for dipping.

Mocha, date, and cinnamon babka

BAKED | PREP + COOK TIME **1 HOUR 20 MINUTES + STANDING** | SERVES **8**

Using dates in this babka adds a caramel-like sweetness that complements and enhances the flavors of chocolate and coffee perfectly. It is best made on the day of serving.

8oz (225g) fresh dates, pitted, chopped

1/3 cup coffee-flavored liqueur

3/4 cup lukewarm milk

2 packages (4 ½ tsp/14g) dried yeast

1/2 cup sugar, divided

2 eggs, lightly beaten

1 egg yolk

3 cups bread flour

3 tsp salt

1/2 cup plus 2 tbsp butter, cubed, softened, plus extra 3 tbsp

1¼ cup dark chocolate (70% cocoa) baking chips

1/2 cup whipping cream

1 tsp instant espresso powder

1/4 cup coarsely chopped walnuts, to garnish

cinnamon chocolate filling

2/3 cup walnuts, lightly toasted, chopped

1/3 cup firmly packed light brown sugar

2 tsp ground cinnamon

3/4 cup dark chocolate (70% cocoa) baking chips

TIP

For step 2, if you don't have an electric mixer with a dough hook, combine the ingredients in a large bowl with a wooden spoon to form a soft dough. Turn out onto a well-floured work surface and knead for 5 minutes until soft and elastic. Knead the butter piece by piece into the dough, kneading well after each addition, until the dough is smooth and elastic.

1 Combine the dates and liqueur in a small bowl. Set aside. In a separate small bowl, combine the milk, yeast, and 1 tablespoon of the sugar. Cover with plastic wrap. Let stand in a warm place for 10 minutes or until frothy. Stir in the egg and egg yolk.

2 In large bowl of an electric mixer fitted with a dough hook attachment, mix the flour, salt, remaining sugar, and yeast mixture on low speed until just combined. Increase speed to medium; mix for 5 minutes until soft and elastic. With the motor operating, gradually add the ½ cup plus 2 tbsp cubed butter, a piece at a time, making sure it's incorporated before adding next piece. Mix until dough is very smooth and elastic. Put in a large oiled bowl; cover with plastic wrap. Let stand in a warm place (but not too warm or dough will be greasy) for 1 hour or until doubled in size.

3 Meanwhile, preheat the oven to 350°F (180°C). Grease a 10-cup tube pan, decorative bundt pan, or kugelhopf pan. Drain the dates, reserving the liqueur. Combine the filling ingredients in a bowl.

4 Punch down dough with your fist. Knead lightly until smooth. On a floured piece of parchment paper, roll out into a rectangle about 12in x 16in (30cm x 40cm) and 1/2in (1cm) thick. Spread extra 3 tbsp butter on dough. Sprinkle evenly with soaked dates and filling. Using the parchment as an aid, roll up firmly from one long side. Using a lightly oiled knife, cut into 12 equal pieces; reshape into rounds. Place 7 pieces, cut-side out, around outer side of the pan. Put remaining pieces of log around the ring of the pan, overlapping slightly. Cover with plastic wrap. Let stand in a warm place for 45 minutes or until dough has almost doubled in size. Bake on lowest oven shelf for 40 minutes or until cooked through. Leave in the pan for 5 minutes, before turning out onto a wire rack to cool slightly.

5 Put the chocolate, cream, coffee granules, and 2 tbsp of the reserved liqueur in a medium microwave-safe bowl. Microwave on high (100%) for 1 minute or until melted and smooth. Let cool for 10 minutes. Serve the warm babka drizzled with the warm mocha sauce and topped with the walnuts.

Warm choc-nut brownie with coffee crème anglaise

BAKED | PREP + COOK TIME **1 HOUR** | SERVES **8**

The light but delicious coffee-flavored crème anglaise served with these brownies makes them extra special. Crème anglaise is a thin pouring custard that's often used with cakes and puddings, as well as with fruit desserts.

12oz (340g) dark chocolate chips, divided (see tips)

$^3/_4$ cup butter, chopped

$^2/_3$ cup sugar

2 eggs, lightly beaten

1$^2/_3$ cup flour

1 tsp baking soda

2 tsp baking powder

1 tsp salt

$^2/_3$ cup coarsely chopped unsalted macadamia nuts, lightly toasted

3.5oz (100g) milk chocolate, coarsely chopped

coffee crème anglaise

2 cups whipping cream

2 tsp instant espresso powder

4 egg yolks

$^1/_4$ cup sugar

TIPS

- These brownies will be only as good as the chocolate used. The more cocoa solids in the chocolate, the more intense the chocolate—and the brownies—will taste.
- The brownies can be made up to 3 days ahead. Store them in an airtight container. Reheat for 30 seconds in the microwave before serving.

1 Preheat the oven to 325°F (170°C). Grease a 9in x 9in (20cm x 20cm) baking dish. Line the bottom with parchment paper.

2 Stir 1$^1/_2$ cups of the dark chocolate with the butter in a medium saucepan over low heat until smooth. Remove from the heat.

3 In a large bowl, combine the sugar, and then the beaten eggs, into the chocolate mixture. Fold in the combined flour, baking soda, baking powder, and salt, then the macadamia nuts, milk chocolate, and the remaining chocolate chips. Spread the brownie mixture over the bottom of the prepared baking dish.

4 Bake for 35 minutes or until a skewer inserted into the center comes out with moist crumbs. Let stand in the baking dish for 10 minutes.

5 Meanwhile, to make the coffee crème anglaise, bring the cream to a boil in a medium saucepan. Remove from the heat. Stir in the coffee until dissolved. Whisk together the egg yolks and sugar in a medium bowl until creamy. Gradually whisk in the warm cream mixture. Return the mixture to the pan. Stir over medium-high heat, without boiling, until the custard thickens and coats the back of a spoon. Strain the custard into a serving container.

6 Serve the brownies warm accompanied by the coffee crème anglaise.

Molten lava cake with quick banana frozen topping

BAKED AND FROZEN | PREP + COOK TIME **50 MINUTES + FREEZING** | SERVES **6**

Due to their high pectin content, bananas naturally have a creamy texture. This is especially noticeable when banana is frozen and blended into a smooth and satisfyingly creamy topping like the one here.

You will need to freeze the bananas a day ahead

1¼ cups flour

1 tsp baking soda

2 tsp baking powder

1 tsp salt

⅓ cup Dutch-process cocoa powder, divided, plus extra, to dust

1 tsp each of ground cinnamon and ground ginger

½ tsp ground nutmeg

¾ cup sugar

1 egg

2 tsp vanilla bean paste or vanilla extract

½ cup milk

2 tbsp almond butter

¾ cup firmly packed light brown sugar

banana frozen topping

1lb (450g) bananas, chopped, frozen (see tips)

1 tsp vanilla bean paste or vanilla extract

4 tbsp pure maple syrup

¼ cup almond butter

TIPS

- You'll need about 2½ large bananas or 3 medium bananas. For accuracy, peel the bananas first, then measure. For the best flavor, use just-ripe bananas.
- Top each serving with finely grated chocolate, if you like.

1 To make the frozen banana topping, put the frozen bananas in the bowl of a food processor. Pulse until coarsely chopped. Add the vanilla bean paste, maple syrup, and almond butter. Process until smooth. Spoon into a 2½-cup (625ml) freezerproof container. Freeze for 2 hours.

2 Preheat the oven to 350°F (180°C). Grease a 7-cup (1.75l) round ovenproof dish. Place on a baking sheet.

3 Sift the flour, baking soda, baking powder, salt, half of the cocoa powder, and the spices into a medium bowl. Stir in the sugar. Whisk together the egg, vanilla bean paste, milk, and almond butter in a small bowl. Add to the dry ingredients; stir until combined. The mixture will be fairly stiff. Add to the prepared baking dish.

4 Combine the brown sugar with the remaining cocoa powder. Sprinkle over the top of the chocolate batter. Slowly pour 1⅓ cups boiling water over the back of a metal spoon to cover the top of the pudding.

5 Bake for 35–45 minutes or until the pudding bounces back when pressed gently in the center.

6 Serve immediately with scoops of the banana frozen topping, dusted with extra cocoa powder.

Stacked mocha blackout cake

BAKED | PREP + COOK TIME **1 HOUR 10 MINUTES + COOLING** | SERVES **10**

With its moist, dense crumb and slathering of intensely chocolaty sour cream frosting, this cake transforms the classic combination of chocolate and coffee into a special-occasion dessert that will excite your guests and definitely satisfy any sweet cravings.

2 tsp instant espresso powder

1¼ cups sugar

1¼ cups light brown sugar

2¼ cups flour

1 cup Dutch-process cocoa powder (see tips)

1 tsp baking soda

2 tsp baking powder

1 tsp salt

⅔ cup vegetable oil

3 eggs, lightly beaten

1 cup buttermilk

unsprayed fresh flowers, to decorate

sour cream chocolate frosting

2 cups powdered sugar

¾ cup Dutch-process cocoa powder

¾ cup plus 2 tbsp unsalted butter, chopped, softened

7oz (200g) dark chocolate (at least 70% cocoa), melted, cooled

1 cup sour cream (see tips)

1 Preheat the oven to 325°F (160°C). Grease 2 deep 9in (20cm) round cake pans. Line the bottoms with parchment paper.

2 Put ½ cup boiling water and the espresso powder in a small bowl. Stir until dissolved. Combine both sugars in a large bowl. Add the sifted flour, cocoa, baking soda, baking powder, and salt. Add the vegetable oil, eggs, buttermilk, and coffee mixture. Whisk to combine. Divide the mixture evenly between the prepared pans (see tips).

3 Bake the cakes for 50–55 minutes or until a skewer inserted into the center comes out clean. Let stand in the pans for 10 minutes before turning out onto wire racks to cool.

4 Meanwhile, to make the sour cream chocolate frosting, sift the powdered sugar and cocoa powder together in a medium bowl. Add the butter. Beat with an electric mixer for 4 minutes or until pale and creamy. Combine the chocolate and sour cream in a separate bowl. Add to the butter mixture. Beat for 2 minutes longer or until stiff.

5 Place one of the cakes, right-side down, on a serving plate. Top with ¾ cup of the chocolate frosting. Spread evenly. Top with the second cake, right-side up, and spread the remaining frosting over the top and side of the cake in large swirls. Decorate with fresh flowers.

TIPS

• Darker and more mellow than natural cocoa powder, Dutch-process cocoa powder is washed during its manufacture to neutralize the natural acidity of cocoa.

• For the frosting, you can substitute 1 cup of full-fat plain Greek yogurt for the sour cream, if you like.

• After putting the batter in the cake pans, weigh them to ensure it's distributed evenly.

NUTS AND CARAMEL

With treats ranging from unctuous caramel fudge to crunchy-topped crumbles, nuts and caramel reign supreme here—whether as a fundamental element or a final flourish.

Chocolate caramel waffle cake

FROZEN | PREP + COOK TIME **30 MINUTES + FREEZING** | SERVES **10**

Premade ingredients are transformed into an almost architectural dessert of irresistible scrumptiousness. This is a great choice for those times when you don't feel like "cooking," and it's sure to impress when you bring it to the table.

You will need to start this recipe a day ahead

2 x 14oz (195g) packages plain or chocolate chip frozen Belgian waffles

2 x 13.4oz (190g) cans dulce de leche

2 x 8oz (113g) packages cream cheese, chopped, softened

4oz (100g) chocolate-dipped sponge candy, coarsely chopped (see page 114)

1¹/₂lb (720g) large navel oranges

¹/₂lb (226g) mandarins or tangerines (see tips)

1 cup premade salted caramel sauce

1 Grease a 9in (24cm) springform pan. Line the bottom and side with baking parchment, extending the parchment 1¹/₄in (3cm) above the edge.

2 Layer the waffles as follows. For the base layer, put a whole waffle in the pan, then place smaller pieces of waffle around it to completely fill in any empty areas. For the second layer, trim the remaining waffles to form a 1in- (2.5cm) wide ring around the inner circumference of the pan, to create a well in the middle.

3 Using an electric mixer, beat together the dulce de leche and the cream cheese in a large bowl until smooth and combined. Fold in half of the chopped chocolate-dipped sponge candy. Spoon the mixture into the waffle-lined pan. Smooth the surface to level. Freeze overnight.

4 The next day, peel the oranges, removing any pith. Slice thinly crosswise, then cut into wedges. Peel and segment the mandarins.

5 To serve, top the waffle cake with the oranges, mandarins, and remaining chocolate-dipped sponge candy. Drizzle with a little of the salted caramel sauce. Serve cut into slices, drizzled with the remaining caramel sauce.

TIPS

- Substitute a honeycomb candy bar (available at some international groceries or online) for the sponge candy, if you'd like.
- If fresh mandarins are unavailable, you can use 8oz (225g) fresh berries or 2 mangoes instead.

Macadamia nut Florentine ice cream sandwiches

BAKED AND FROZEN | PREP + COOK TIME **45 MINUTES PLUS COOLING + FREEZING** | SERVES **6**

Florentines are typically made with nuts and candied fruit, but these Florentines use nuts and dried fruit including macadamias, dried cranberries, and crystallized ginger. If you're short on time, use premade Florentines instead.

6 tbsp butter

³/₄ cup sugar

1 tsp salt

1¹/₄ cup whipping cream

³/₄ cup flour

¹/₄ tsp ground ginger

³/₄ cup coarsely chopped macadamia nuts

¹/₄ cup dried cranberries

¹/₄ cup crystallized ginger, coarsely chopped

1 cup dark chocolate chips

1 pint (473 ml) slightly softened vanilla ice cream (see tips)

1   Preheat the oven to 325°F (160°C). Line two large baking sheets with parchment paper.

2   Melt the butter in a medium saucepan over medium heat. Add the sugar, salt, and whipping cream. Cook, stirring, for 2 minutes or until well combined. Fold in the flour and ground ginger; be careful not to overmix. Remove from the heat.

3   Once the mixture is cool enough to handle, and working in batches, drop 2 tablespoons of the mixture on top of each other onto the prepared baking sheets, leaving a 1¹/₄in (3cm) gap between each one. The mixture should spread to a 3¹/₄in (8cm) round and make 12 rounds in total. Sprinkle the macadamia nuts, cranberries, and crystallized ginger evenly over the rounds.

4   Bake for 22 minutes or until light golden in the center, rotating the baking sheets during cooking so that the cookies brown evenly. Let cool on the baking sheets. They will harden as they cool.

5   Microwave the chocolate in a small bowl on high (100%) in 30-second bursts, stirring well, until melted. Allow to cool slightly. Set aside.

6   To assemble, scoop the slightly softened ice cream into 6 large balls. Sandwich 1 scoop between 2 Florentines, placing the cookies topping-side out. Gently press the cookies together to form even sandwiches. Dip each sandwich a third of the way down into the melted chocolate. Arrange on a tray. Freeze until the chocolate sets.

7   Serve the ice cream sandwiches straight from the freezer.

TIPS

• Use salted caramel or butter pecan ice cream instead of vanilla, if you like.

• The Florentines can be made up to 3 days ahead. Store in an airtight container or freeze for up to 3 months.

Peanut butter cakes

BAKED | PREP + COOK TIME **35 MINUTES** | MAKES **6**

Using crunchy peanut butter instead of smooth adds wonderful texture to these gooey cakes with pops of chocolate, ginger, and peanut goodness in every bite. They'll last a day or two in the fridge if they don't get gobbled up immediately. Reheat for 30 seconds in the microwave.

6 eggs

2.5oz (75g) dark chocolate (70% cocoa), divided

$3/4$ cup crystallized ginger (see tips)

$1/2$ cup sugar

$1^1/2$ cups crunchy peanut butter (see tips)

$1/2$ tsp salt

$2/3$ cup whipping cream

2 tsp powdered sugar, sifted

1 Preheat the oven to 375°F (190°C). Grease six $3/4$-cup (180ml) ramekins ,or ovenproof dishes.

2 Separate the eggs. Put the egg whites in a small cup or bowl and the yolks in the bowl of an electric mixer. Finely chop two-thirds of the chocolate. Finely chop the crystallized ginger. Reserve 2 tablespoons for serving.

3 In a large bowl, add the sugar to the egg yolks. Beat with an electric mixer until light and creamy. Blend the peanut butter and $1/3$ cup boiling water separately. Add to the egg yolk mixture. Beat until combined. Stir in the chopped chocolate, crystallized ginger, and salt.

4 Carefully wash and thoroughly dry the bowl of the electric mixer. Add the egg whites to the clean bowl. Beat with the electric mixer until soft peaks form. (Any fat or moisture in the bowl will prevent the egg whites from forming peaks.) Fold one-third of the egg whites into the batter, in 3 batches, until combined. Spoon the mixture into ramekins.

5 Bake the cakes for 20 minutes or until gooey in the center.

6 Meanwhile, finely grate the remaining chocolate or shave it with a peeler. Beat the whipping cream and sifted powdered sugar with an electric mixer to form soft peaks.

7 Serve the puddings immediately, topped with whipped cream, the reserved ginger, and the grated chocolate.

TIPS

- Instead of crystallized ginger, you can use the same weight of chopped fresh dates or dried figs.
- Use a major brand of peanut butter with sweeteners added. Natural peanut butters won't yield the same result.
- Serve the cakes drizzled with dulce de leche or topped with vanilla ice cream, if you like.

Orange crème caramel with hazelnut brittle

BAKED | PREP + COOK TIME **1 HOUR + OVERNIGHT REFRIGERATION** | SERVES **12**

Sometimes you just need to go with a retro favorite, and this crème caramel with a twist fits the bill. The custard base is made with condensed milk in the style of a Latin American flan, while the strong, deep flavor of the hazelnut brittle pairs particularly well with the orange.

You will need to start this recipe a day ahead

cooking oil spray for greasing

1¼ cups sugar, divided

1½ lb (600g) oranges

14oz (396g) can sweetened condensed milk

2½ cups whole milk

6 eggs

½ cup skinless toasted hazelnuts, coarsely chopped (see tips)

heavy cream, for serving (optional)

TIPS

• If you can't find toasted hazelnuts, roast your hazelnuts in the oven for 10 minutes, then wrap in a clean tea towel. Allow to steam for a minute, then rub off the skins with the hazelnuts still wrapped in the tea towel.

• You can use other nuts such as almonds or cashews instead of hazelnuts.

1 Lightly coat a 9in x 9in (18cm x 18cm) baking dish with cooking oil spray.

2 Put 1 cup of sugar and ½ cup water in a small saucepan. Stir over medium heat without boiling until sugar dissolves. Bring to a boil without stirring. Boil softly 8 minutes or until golden brown. Pour caramel into baking dish. Carefully swirl it to coat bottom and sides.

3 Preheat the oven to 325°F (160°). Cut the zest from 1 of the oranges in long, thin strips; reserve. Finely grate the zest of the other orange (you will need 2 tablespoons).

4 Whisk together both milks, eggs, and 1 tablespoon of grated orange zest in a large bowl until combined. Strain mixture directly onto the caramel. Place baking dish in a roasting pan large enough to hold it with room on all sides. Place roasting pan and crème caramel in the oven. Add enough hot water to roasting pan to come halfway up the sides of the baking dish. Be careful not to splash any hot water into the crème caramel.

5 Bake the crème caramel for 45 minutes. The mixture will still be wobbly in the center. Carefully remove baking dish from water. Using your fingers, gently pull the custard away from the sides; this prevents the top of the custard from cracking as it cools. Cover and refrigerate overnight.

6 Line a baking sheet with baking parchment. Put the remaining ¼ cup sugar and 1 tablespoon water in a small heavy-based saucepan. Cook, stirring, over low heat until the sugar dissolves. Add the remaining grated orange zest; increase the heat to high. Cook without stirring for 6 minutes or until golden. Remove the pan from the heat. Quickly stir in the hazelnuts to coat. Pour onto the lined sheet. Let cool completely. Break or coarsely chop the hazelnut brittle into pieces.

7 Place a serving platter with a lip right-side down on the baking dish holding the crème caramel. Quickly invert the pan so the dessert drops onto the platter. Serve topped with the reserved strips of orange zest and hazelnut brittle, as well as heavy cream, if you like.

Little mandarin and almond crater cakes

BAKED | PREP + COOK TIME **3 HOURS + COOLING** | MAKES **12**

The craters in these moist, citrus-dense almond cakes create the ideal little vessels to spoon thick yogurt, custard, or even ice cream into for serving. Candied zest tops off these mini mandarin-fests with a zesty flourish.

2lb (1 kg) whole mandarin oranges or tangerines

3¹/₄ cups sliced almonds, divided

6 eggs

1¹/₂ cups sugar, divided

1¹/₂ tsp baking powder

1 tsp salt

1 cup Greek yogurt, for serving

TIPS

• The mandarin purée and candied zest can be made a day ahead. Store the purée in the fridge and the zest at room temperature.

• In step 5, you can add 1 teaspoon vanilla extract to the cake mixture, if you like.

1 Place 2 whole mandarins in a medium saucepan with enough water to cover. Bring to a boil. Reduce the heat to low. Simmer for 30 minutes, adding more water as needed to keep the mandarins covered at all times. Remove from the water; let cool. Split open; remove and discard the seeds. Add the mandarins—including the peel—to the food processor and purée into a paste.

2 Preheat the oven to 350°F (180°C).

3 Line two baking sheets with parchment paper. Divide 2¹/₂ cups of the almonds evenly between the baking sheets. Roast for 7 minutes, stirring halfway through the cooking time, or until golden. Let cool, then process to fine crumbs.

4 Spray the insides of a 12-hole (³/₄ cup) muffin pan.

5 Using an electric mixer, beat the eggs and 1 cup of sugar in a large bowl for 10 minutes or until thick, pale, and tripled in volume. Fold in the ground almonds, mandarin purée, baking powder, and salt. Spoon into muffin pan, dividing between the 12 holes. Top with remaining almonds.

6 Bake the cakes for 30 minutes or until they look set and have come away from the edge and sunk slightly in the center. Leave in the pan for 10 minutes. Transfer to a wire rack to cool completely.

7 Meanwhile, remove the zest and any pith from the remaining mandarins. Slice the zest into thin strips. Remove the segments from the mandarins and add to the food processor; process the mandarin segments until smooth. Pour the purée through a strainer over a measuring cup; discard the pulp. You should have about ²/₃ cup juice. Top off with water to make 1 cup. Put the juice mixture and remaining sugar in a small saucepan over low heat. Stir without boiling until the sugar dissolves. Add the zest. Boil for 5 minutes or until golden. Transfer the zest to a baking sheet lined with parchment paper. Let cool. Serve the cakes with the candied mandarin zest and yogurt.

Almond crumble tray-baked fruit

BAKED | PREP + COOK TIME **1 HOUR 20 MINUTES** | SERVES **6**

The humble crumble is a very versatile and forgiving dessert. Swap and use your favorite fruit such as apple, raspberries, or plums within the same quantities—just be sure to adjust the cooking time and cook until the fruit is tender.

2½ lb (1.2 kg) bosc pears

8oz (225g) blackberries, plus extra, to garnish (see tips)

1lb (600g) navel oranges

⅓ cup sugar, divided

6 tbsp butter

1 cup slivered almonds

1 cup rolled (old-fashioned) oats

1 Preheat the oven to 400°F (200°C).

2 Halve and core the pears. Cut each half into 4 wedges. Arrange the pears and blackberries in an 8-cup (2l) ovenproof dish.

3 Remove the zest from 1 of the oranges using a zesting tool. Finely grate the zest from the second orange. Reserve the zests separately. Squeeze the oranges; you will need ¾ cup orange juice. Pour the juice over the pears in the dish. Sprinkle with half of the sugar and the first batch of reserved strips of zest. Stir to coat.

4 Bake the fruit, stirring occasionally, for 45 minutes or until the pears are almost tender.

5 Meanwhile, finely chop the butter. Put the almonds, rolled oats, remaining sugar, and chopped butter in a medium bowl. Using your fingertips, work the butter into the almond mixture with both hands until the mixture resembles coarse crumbs.

6 Scatter the almond crumbs over the pear mixture. Bake for 15 minutes or until the crumble is golden. Serve topped with the extra blackberries and the second batch of reserved grated zest.

TIPS

- Use frozen berries when fresh blackberries are not in season.
- Serve with scoops of vanilla ice cream.

Salted caramels

STOVETOP | PREP + COOK TIME **30 MINUTES + COOLING** | MAKES **40**

Adding salt flakes to these simple caramels turns them into a taste sensation in your mouth. Making your own caramels is not a daunting process. Just be patient and make sure the syrup mixture reaches the right temperature before taking it off the heat.

1½ cups sugar

1½ cups heavy cream

¼ cup light corn syrup

2 tsp sea salt flakes

1 Grease a 9in x 9in (20cm x 20cm) baking dish. Line the bottom and sides with parchment paper, extending the parchment 2in (5cm) over the sides.

2 Stir the sugar, heavy cream, and corn syrup in a medium saucepan over medium heat until the sugar dissolves. Bring to a boil. Boil until the mixture reaches 248°F (120°C) on a candy thermometer (firm-ball stage). As soon as it reaches this temperature, remove the pan from the heat. Sprinkle in 1 teaspoon of the salt flakes; do not stir.

3 Pour the caramel into the lined baking dish. Sprinkle with the remaining salt. Let cool.

4 Use a warm, sharp oiled knife to cut the caramel into squares. Wrap in waxed paper or serve in little paper cases.

Caramel candy variations

Home-made candy can be hard to resist, and the examples here are no exception. Make them as festive treats or to give as gifts to family and friends—or make them simply for the sheer indulgence of enjoying them yourself, no special occasion needed.

Almond and chocolate brittle

Grease a shallow 6in x 9in (18cm x 28cm) pan or dish. Make the salted caramels as described on page 98, adding 1½ cups roasted almonds and 2½oz (75g) finely chopped dark chocolate with 1 teaspoon salt flakes once the mixture reaches 240°F (110°C) on a candy thermometer. Stir until the mixture reaches 284°F (140°C). Pour into the prepared pan. Sprinkle with 1 teaspoon salt flakes. Let cool. Cut into triangles. The candy will harden as it cools.

Macadamia nut brittle

Grease a shallow 6in x 9in (18cm x 28cm) pan or dish. Make the salted caramels as described on page 98, adding 1½ cups unsalted roasted macadamia nuts and 1 teaspoon salt flakes once the mixture reaches 284°F (140°C) on a candy thermometer. Pour into the prepared pan. Sprinkle with 1 teaspoon salt flakes. Let cool. Break the brittle into pieces with your hands.

Eggnog caramels

Make the salted caramels as described on page 98, omitting the salt and adding 1½ teaspoons ground cinnamon, ¼ teaspoon ground nutmeg, a pinch of ground cloves, 1 teaspoon vanilla extract, and 2 tablespoons white rum to the pan with the sugar. Continue as directed in the recipe.

Earl Grey caramels

Infuse 2 Earl Grey teabags in ¾ cup boiling water. Remove the teabags, pressing with a spoon to release all the liquid. Make the salted caramels as described on page 98, omitting the salt and adding the tea to the sugar, cream, and corn syrup in the pan. Continue as directed in the recipe.

Coconut banoffee tart

SET | PREP + COOK TIME **25 MINUTES + REFRIGERATION** | SERVES **8**

Known as "banoffee," this custardy pie filling combines the salty caramel of toffee with the sweet richness of bananas—a classic combination in many countries. This version is on a delicious cookie crust and topped with coconut flakes and caramelized bananas.

10oz (280g) Biscoff cookies or sugar cookies

³/₄ cup butter, divided

2 cups mascarpone, divided

13.4oz (380g) can dulce de leche

¹/₂ tsp sea salt flakes

1lb (460g) bananas, just ripe

2 tbsp sugar

¹/₄ cup unsweetened coconut flakes

1   Grease a 9in (24cm) round tart pan with removable bottom.

2   In a food processor, crush the cookies into fine crumbs. Melt ½ cup of the butter in a small saucepan or in a heatproof bowl in the microwave. Stir in the cookie crumbs. Press over the base and side of the tart pan. Refrigerate for 1 hour or overnight until firm.

3   Put 1 cup of the mascarpone, the dulce de leche, and salt in a large bowl. Whisk until smooth and soft peaks form. Spread over the cookie base. Refrigerate for 2 hours.

4   Melt the remaining butter in a large nonstick skillet over high heat. Thickly slice the bananas lengthwise. Sprinkle with the sugar. Cook the bananas for 30 seconds on each side or until caramelized (see tips).

5   Top the tart with the caramelized banana and coconut chips. Serve with the remaining mascarpone.

TIPS

- The cookie crust can be made a day ahead. Refrigerate until needed.
- The tart can be made to the end of step 3 the day before. Cover and refrigerate. Cook the bananas just before serving.
- In step 4, you can use a kitchen blowtorch, if you own one, to caramelize the bananas.

Spanish caramel orange cake

BAKED | PREP + COOK TIME **1 HOUR 25 MINUTES + STANDING** | SERVES **8**

Dulce de leche, the Latin American caramel, is made by simmering sweetened milk until thick and caramelized. Used here in combination with cream as a filling and topping, it transforms a simple butter cake into an afternoon-tea delight.

1½ cups (3 sticks) butter, softened, plus extra for greasing

2 tsp vanilla bean paste (see tips)

2 cups sugar, plus extra 2 tbsp

4 eggs, room temperature

3 cups flour, sifted

2 tsp baking powder

1 tsp baking soda

1 tsp salt

1⅓ cups milk

1 tbsp lemon juice

¾ cup strained orange juice

1 cup marscapone

1 cup dulce de leche (see tips)

1½ lb (700g) blood oranges, peeled, thinly sliced

¼ cup sliced almonds, roasted

1 Preheat the oven to 325°F (160°C). Grease 2 deep 9in (20cm) round cake pans. Line the bottoms with parchment paper.

2 Using an electric mixer, beat the butter, vanilla, and 2 cups of sugar in a medium bowl until light and fluffy. Add the eggs, one at a time, beating between additions until just combined. Fold in the flour, baking powder, baking soda, salt, and milk in two batches. Divide the mixture evenly between the 2 prepared pans, spreading over the bottom of each pan.

3 Bake the cakes for 50–55 minutes or until a skewer inserted into the center comes out clean. Let the cakes cool in the pans for 10 minutes before turning onto a wire rack to cool completely.

4 Put the extra 2 tablespoons sugar and the lemon and orange juices in a medium saucepan. Stir over medium heat until the sugar dissolves. Bring to a boil. Boil for 5 minutes or until the syrup thickens slightly and reduces to ⅓ cup. Transfer the syrup to a small bowl. Cool quickly by placing in a bowl of iced water for 10 minutes.

5 Meanwhile, whisk together the mascarpone and dulce de leche in a medium bowl until soft peaks form.

6 Remove the parchment from the bottom of each cake. Split each cooled cake in half horizontally, so that you have 4 layers. Place one cake layer, cut-side up, on a cake plate. Brush with 1 tablespoon of the cooled orange syrup. Spread with one-quarter of the dulce de leche cream. Repeat the layers 3 more times with the remaining cake, orange syrup, and dulce de leche cream.

7 Top the cake with half of the sliced oranges, and sprinkle with the almonds. Serve the cake accompanied by the remaining orange slices.

TIPS

- You can substitute the same amount of vanilla extract for the vanilla bean paste.
- Dulce de leche is available in cans. You will find it in the baking aisle of your local grocery store.

Sugar and spice almonds

ROASTED | PREP + COOK TIME **30 MINUTES + COOLING** | MAKES **5 CUPS**

These sweet, spicy almonds are great as a snack or to serve to guests. You can even present them as gifts, wrapped in a gift bag with a decorative ribbon tied at the top. The cinnamon sugar caramelizes slightly in the oven, adding a crisp coating to the crunchy almonds.

1½ cups powdered sugar

1½ tbsp ground cinnamon

5 cups almonds

1 Preheat the oven to 350°F (180°C). Line two baking sheets with parchment paper.

2 Sift the sugar and cinnamon together twice into a medium bowl. Put the almonds in a colander. Rinse under cold water. Tip the wet almonds out onto the prepared baking sheets. Sift the cinnamon mixture over the almonds. Toss to coat.

3 Roast for 20 minutes, stirring halfway through the cooking time, or until fragrant and browned. Let cool on the baking sheets; they will become crisp upon cooling. Separate the almonds, then store them in airtight jars or pack them in cellophane or similar gift bags, sealing the bags tightly at the top to ensure the nuts retain their freshness.

Pear fritters with raspberry and rose syrup

FRIED | PREP + COOK TIME **20 MINUTES** | SERVES **4**

Using purchased pancake mix is a speedy and fail-proof hack for these tender-crisp fritters. The textural and flavor contrasts between the crisp batter coating and the sweet, fragrant pears provide an object lesson in perfect pairings, finished with the crunch of pistachios.

$^3/_4$ cup premade pancake batter (see tips)

$^1/_4$ cup vegetable oil

1lb (460g) firm pears, peeled, cored, thickly sliced

2–3 tbsp fresh raspberries

$^1/_3$ cup honey

1 tsp rose water

$^1/_3$ cup Greek yogurt

2 tbsp coarsely chopped raw pistachios

1   If using a dry mix, make the pancake batter according to the instructions. Pour the batter into a small bowl.

2   Heat 1 tablespoon of the vegetable oil in a large frying pan over medium heat.

3   Add the pear slices to the pancake batter. Fry the coated pear slices in batches, adding more oil in between, for 2 minutes on each side or until golden. Drain on paper towels.

4   Put the raspberries, honey, and rose water in a small bowl. Mash with a fork to combine and crush.

5   Divide the warm fritters among 4 serving bowls. Top with the yogurt and raspberry rose syrup. Sprinkle with the pistachios.

TIPS

- You can easily find dry pancake mix or the liquid mix at your grocery store.
- Any leftover pancake batter can be stored in the fridge and used the following day.

Amaretti crumbles with apple and cherry

BAKED | PREP + COOK TIME **35 MINUTES** | SERVES **4**

Almond-flavored amaretti cookies complement the cherries beautifully here, transforming the humble crumble into something oh-so-special. If you aren't a fan of amaretti, however, you can use another cookie instead. Shortbread works equally well in this recipe.

1½ lb (750kg) firm red apples, such as honeycrisp, peeled, cored, and thickly sliced

¼ cup sugar

½ tsp salt

½ tsp cinnamon

¼ tsp allspice

½ tsp nutmeg

1½ cups frozen cherries (see tip)

5oz (150g) amaretti cookies, crushed

¼ cup almond meal

¼ cup slivered almonds

¼ cup flour

6 tbsp cold butter, finely chopped, plus extra for greasing

vanilla ice cream, for serving (optional)

1   Preheat the oven to 400°F (200°C). Grease four 1¼-cup (310ml) ovenproof dishes.

2   Combine the apples, sugar, 2 tablespoons water, salt, cinnamon, allspice, and nutmeg in a medium saucepan. Cook, covered, over medium heat for about 5 minutes or until the apples are just tender. Remove from the heat. Stir in the cherries. Divide the mixture among the prepared dishes.

3   Meanwhile, combine the crushed cookies, almond meal, slivered almonds, and flour in a medium bowl. Work the cold butter into the dry ingredients with both hands until large, heavy crumbs form. Sprinkle the mixture evenly over the apple-cherry mixture.

4   Place the dishes on a baking sheet. Bake for about 20 minutes or until browned. Serve with ice cream, if you like.

TIP

Instead of the cherries, you can use any frozen berry you like.

Skillet cake with tahini maple caramel pears

BAKED | PREP + COOK TIME **40 MINUTES** | SERVES **6**

Roasted pears and maple syrup make this recipe a sublime choice for an autumnal weekend brunch. It can also serve as an everyday family dessert, especially when it takes advantage of seasonal fruit. Quick and easy, it's even more perfect with vanilla ice cream.

1³/₄ cups flour

1 tsp baking soda

1½ tsp baking powder

½ tsp salt

2 tsp ground cinnamon, divided

¹/₃ cup tahini, divided

²/₃ cup maple syrup, divided

2 eggs, lightly beaten

1¹/₂ cups buttermilk

4 tbsp butter, divided

1¹/₂ lb (690g) firm Bosc pears, unpeeled, cut into wedges

2 tbsp lemon juice

toasted sesame seeds, to garnish

1   Preheat the oven to 425°F (220°C). Place a 10in (26cm) (top measurement) ovenproof skillet in the oven to preheat.

2   Put the flour, baking powder, baking soda, salt, and 1 teaspoon of the cinnamon in a large bowl. Add 2 tablespoons each of the tahini and maple syrup, then add the egg and buttermilk. Whisk until combined.

3   Heat 2 tbsp of the butter in a separate large skillet over medium heat. Add the pears. Cook, turning occasionally, for 8 minutes or until browned and almost tender. Add the remaining cinnamon, tahini, and maple syrup, then the lemon juice. Stir gently until combined. Cook, over low heat, stirring occasionally, for 5 minutes or until the pears are tender and the sauce has thickened. Set aside.

4   Meanwhile, carefully but quickly remove the hot skillet from the oven. Add the remaining butter; swirl to coat. Pour in the batter. Smooth the surface. Bake for 15 minutes or until puffed and browned.

5   To serve, top the hot skillet cake with the tahini maple caramel pears, and sprinkle with the sesame seeds.

TIP

You could also make individual pancakes with this mixture, if you like.

Warm chocolate caramel pavlovas

BAKED | PREP + COOK TIME **40 MINUTES** | SERVES **4**

Designed to impress, this meringue recipe foregoes the more typical fresh fruit and uses a delectable combination of banana, salted caramel, and chocolate instead. The sponge candy on top is the icing on the cake—or pavlova, in this case.

2 egg whites

1^1/$_3$ cups powdered sugar

1 tbsp cocoa powder, sifted

1 cup salted caramel dessert sauce

2 bananas

1^1/$_4$ cups heavy cream

chocolate-dipped sponge candy

1 cup sugar

^{1}/$_3$ cup light corn syrup

1 tbsp vinegar

1 tbsp baking soda

sea salt flakes for sprinkling

melted milk chocolate for dipping

1 To make the chocolate-dipped sponge candy, line a baking sheet with baking parchment.

2 Stir together the sugar, corn syrup, vinegar, and ^{1}/$_4$ cup water in a medium heavy-based saucepan over low heat until the sugar dissolves. Increase the heat to medium; boil, without stirring, for 8–9 minutes until the syrup is a dark golden honey color or until it reaches 325°F (160°C) (hard-crack stage) on a candy thermometer. Immediately remove the pan from the heat and stir in the baking soda—the syrup will froth.

3 As soon as the last of the soda dissolves, carefully and quickly pour the honeycomb onto the prepared baking sheet; don't spread the mixture or it will deflate. Sprinkle with salt; let cool to room temperature.

4 Break the cooled sponge candy into chunks. Dip the pieces into the chocolate and return to the baking sheet. Let stand until set.

5 To make the pavlovas, preheat the oven to 350°F (180°C). Line a baking sheet with baking parchment.

6 Using an electric mixer, beat the egg whites, powdered sugar, and ^{1}/$_3$ cup boiling water in a small bowl for about 10 minutes or until firm peaks form.

7 Fold the sifted cocoa into the meringue. Drop 4 equal amounts of the mixture onto the lined tray. Use the back of a spoon to create a well in the center of each mound. Bake for 25 minutes or until firm to the touch.

8 Meanwhile, heat the caramel sauce according to the directions on the bottle or jar. Just before serving, peel and thinly slice the bananas.

9 Serve the pavlovas straight from the oven, topped with the warm caramel sauce, sliced banana, cream, and chocolate-dipped sponge candy.

TIPS

▪ You can make the sponge candy in advance and store it in an airtight container.
▪ You can substitute a honeycomb candy bar (available at some international groceries and online) for the sponge candy, if you'd like.

114

Pecan, macadamia nut, and walnut tartlets

BAKED | PREP + COOK TIME **2 HOURS 15 MINUTES** | MAKES **4**

With their buttery almond pastry filled to the brim with a mixture of pecans, macadamia nuts, and walnuts sweetened with maple syrup, these tartlets are a nut-lover's dream. Make sure to use nuts that are fresh so that the filling is as crunchy and flavorful as possible.

1¹/₄ cups flour

¹/₃ cup powdered sugar

¹/₄ cup almond flour

¹/₂ tsp salt

¹/₂ cup cold butter, coarsely chopped, plus extra for greasing

1 egg yolk

filling

¹/₃ cup toasted macadamia nuts

¹/₃ cup toasted pecans

¹/₃ cup toasted walnuts

2 tbsp light brown sugar

1 tbsp flour

3 tbsp butter, melted

2 eggs

³/₄ cup pure maple syrup

1 In a food processor, process the flour, powdered sugar, almond flour, and salt with the cold butter until combined. Add the egg yolk and process until the ingredients just come together. Knead the dough on a floured work surface until smooth. Wrap with plastic wrap; refrigerate for 30 minutes.

2 Grease four 4in (10cm) loose-bottomed fluted mini tart pans. Divide the pie dough into 4 equal portions. Roll out each portion between sheets of parchment paper until large enough to line the pans. Lift the pie dough into the pans. Press into the bases and sides; trim the edges. Cover, then refrigerate for 1 hour.

3 Preheat the oven to 400°F (200°C).

4 Place the tart pans on a baking sheet. Line the pie dough in each with baking parchment; fill with dried beans or rice. Bake blind for 10 minutes. Remove the parchment and beans. Bake for 7 minutes longer or until lightly browned. Let cool.

5 Reduce the oven temperature to 350°F (180°C).

6 To make the filling, combine all the ingredients in a medium bowl. Spoon into the pie crusts.

7 Bake the tartlets for about 25 minutes. Let cool.

Almond and apricot phyllo tarte Tatin

BAKED | PREP + COOK TIME **50 MINUTES** | SERVES **4**

In the traditional tarte Tatin, the apples are baked before being topped with pastry.
Using canned fruit is a quick way of making this variant of the impressive French dessert.
It speeds up the cooking time, which always helps!

1 tbsp butter

$^1/_3$ cup firmly packed light brown sugar

1 vanilla pod, split lengthwise, seeds scraped

4 sheets of phyllo dough (thawed if frozen)

2 x 15oz (425g) cans apricot halves in juice, drained

2 tbsp sliced almonds

extra virgin olive oil cooking oil spray

whipped cream, for serving (see tip)

1 Preheat the oven to 400°F (200°C).

2 Combine the butter, sugar, vanilla pod and seeds, and 2 tablespoons water in a medium ovenproof skillet (with a base measurement of 10in [25cm]) over medium heat. Cook, stirring, for 1 minute or until the butter is melted and the sugar has dissolved.

3 Increase the heat to high. Cook, stirring occasionally, for 2 minutes or until the liquid has thickened slightly.

4 Meanwhile, put 1 sheet of phyllo dough on your work surface. Spray with the olive oil cooking spray. Top with another pastry sheet, placed perpendicular to the first. Spray with the olive oil. Top with another pastry sheet, placing it diagonally over the previous one. Spray again with the olive oil. Top with the remaining pastry sheet, in the opposite diagonal direction. Spray with the olive oil.

5 Arrange the apricots in the skillet with the sauce, covering the bottom of the pan but leaving a narrow border empty of fruit; sprinkle the nuts over only the fruit. Place the pastry, sprayed-side up, over the apricots; carefully tuck in the pastry all around the edge of the skillet.

6 Bake for 20 minutes or until the pastry is golden and crisp. Carefully turn onto a serving plate. Cut into wedges, discarding the vanilla pod. Serve warm with whipped cream for dolloping over the top.

TIP

Instead of whipped cream, you could serve the tart with vanilla ice cream or Greek yogurt.

SPICES
AND HERBS

Refreshing, fragrant, soothing, warming,
earthy, exotic—look no further than these
aromatic, tempting treats when you need
a little spice in your life.

Caramel ginger muffins with butterscotch sauce

BAKED | PREP + COOK TIME **1 HOUR** | SERVES **6**

With an indulgent butterscotch sauce and a double dose of warming ginger, this inviting treat
is sure to satisfy any sweet craving. You can make the muffins and butterscotch sauce ahead
of time, then reheat them when you are ready to serve.

1 cup sugar, divided

1/2 cup butter, softened

2 tsp ground ginger

2 eggs

1 2/3 cup flour

1 tsp baking soda

1 tsp baking powder

1/2 tsp salt

1/2 cup crystallized ginger, finely chopped, divided

1/2 cup milk

butterscotch sauce

3/4 cup plus 2 tbsp butter, chopped

1 1/4 cups heavy cream

3/4 cup firmly packed brown sugar

TIPS

• To reheat, simply microwave each muffin
for 20 seconds on high. Increase the time to
2 minutes to reheat the entire batch.

• The muffins can be made a day ahead and
stored in an airtight container.

• The butterscotch sauce can be made up
to a week ahead. Keep it refrigerated.

• Both the muffins and the sauce can be
frozen separately for up to 3 months. Thaw
both before reheating.

• Serve the muffins with ice cream, if you like.

1 Grease 9 holes of a standard (1/2 cup) muffin pan. Or, if you'd prefer, line
them with paper baking cups.

2 Put 1/2 cup of the sugar in a small saucepan over medium-high heat.
Cook, swirling the pan often, for 3 minutes or until the sugar is a deep
golden color. Remove from the heat. Carefully pour in 1/2 cup water all at
once—the mixture will bubble fiercely. Return to the heat. Cook for
3 minutes longer or until the caramel has mostly dissolved. Let stand
for 5 minutes.

3 Meanwhile, using an electric mixer, beat the butter, remaining 1/2 cup
sugar, and ground ginger in a small bowl until light and fluffy. Beat in
1 egg at a time. Working in 2 batches, fold in the flour, baking soda,
baking powder, salt, and 1/3 cup of the crystallized ginger, then the milk
and the cooled caramel.

4 Divide the mixture evenly among the holes of the muffin tin. Bake the
muffins for 30 minutes or until a toothpick inserted into the centers
comes out clean. Turn out onto a wire rack.

5 Meanwhile, to make the butterscotch sauce, combine the ingredients in
a medium saucepan. Stir over medium heat until the butter melts. Bring
to a boil. Simmer for 3 minutes.

6 Serve the warm muffins drizzled with the butterscotch sauce, and
topped with the remaining crystallized ginger.

Rose- and cardamom-soaked doughnuts

FRIED | PREP + COOK TIME **40 MINUTES + STANDING** | SERVES **6**

Soaked in a fragrant rose water syrup for extra sweetness, and redolent of the tastes and aromas of the Middle East, these fluffy bite-sized doughnuts are the treat you've been dreaming of. Serve with fresh fruit, such as sliced mango, orange, or strawberries, if you like.

1 tsp dried yeast

2 egg yolks

3 1/2 cups flour

1 tsp ground cardamom

6 tbsp butter, chopped, softened

2 1/4 cups sugar, divided

3 large lemons

1/2 cup rose water

vegetable oil for deep-frying

1 Put 1 1/4 cups lukewarm water in a small bowl. Whisk in the yeast and egg yolks. Put the flour, cardamom, chopped butter, and yeast mixture in the bowl of an electric mixer. Using the paddle attachment, beat for 4 minutes or until the dough is smooth and elastic. Cover the bowl. Let stand in a warm place for 1 hour or until the dough has doubled in size.

2 Meanwhile, put 1 cup water and 2 cups of the sugar in a small saucepan. Stir over low heat, without boiling, until the sugar dissolves. Bring to a boil. Cook for 5 minutes, without stirring, or until the syrup thickens slightly.

3 Remove the zest from 2 lemons using a zesting tool. Juice both of the lemons; you will need 1/2 cup juice. Add the lemon zest, lemon juice, and rose water to the syrup. Remove from the heat. Cover to keep warm. Finely grate the zest from the remaining lemon. Reserve.

4 Place a wire rack on a baking sheet. Fill a large saucepan one-third full of vegetable oil. Heat to 325°F (160°C) (or until a cube of bread turns golden in 30 seconds when dropped into the hot oil). Deep-fry heaped tablespoons of the dough, in batches, until lightly browned and cooked through. Drain on the wire rack.

5 Pour the warm syrup over the hot doughnuts. Sprinkle with the reserved lemon zest. Serve immediately.

TIPS

- As you fry, you may need to adjust the heat under the pan to keep the oil at an even temperature.
- The leftover syrup makes a refreshing cordial mixture, or freeze it and make a granita or sorbet.
- You can use orange blossom water instead of rose water, if you like.

Churros ravioli with chocolate and ice cream

FRIED | PREP + COOK TIME **30 MINUTES** | SERVES **4**

Wonton wrappers aren't just for savory applications. The dough consists of only flour, eggs, and water, so it can easily be transformed. Here the wrappers are used to make sweet fried ravioli, and given a churros twist with chocolate filling and cinnamon sugar.

24 square or round wonton wrappers

12 pre-made chocolate truffles (see tips)

1 tbsp sugar

1 tsp cinnamon

vegetable oil for deep-frying

$^1/_2$ cup cherry jam (see tips)

1 cup vanilla ice cream

1 Place 12 wonton wrappers on a clean surface. Working on one at a time, put 1 chocolate truffle in the center of each wrapper. Brush the edges of the wrapper with a little water. Top with another wrapper; press the edges together firmly (see tips).

2 In a small bowl, combine the sugar and cinnamon until mixed.

3 Heat enough vegetable oil for deep-frying in a medium saucepan over medium heat until it reaches 325°F (170°C) (or until a cube of bread dropped into the hot oil sizzles and browns in 20 seconds). Gently fry the ravioli, in batches, for 1$^1/_2$ minutes or until golden. Remove each batch with a slotted spoon; drain on a tray lined with paper towels. Dust with the cinnamon sugar.

4 Put the cherry jam in a small saucepan with 2 tablespoons water. Stir over low heat until melted and smooth.

5 Serve the warm ravioli with scoops of ice cream and the warmed jam.

TIPS

- Choose your favorite type of chocolate truffles to fill the ravioli.
- You can use marmalade instead of the cherry jam, if you like.
- In step 1, make sure to press out all the air pockets. The ravioli should be completely sealed at the edges; any little gaps will allow melted chocolate to leak out during cooking.
- The ravioli can be made to the end of step 1 up to 4 hours ahead. Store, covered, in the fridge until needed.
- Any leftover wonton wrappers can be tightly wrapped in plastic wrap and frozen for up to 1 month.

Cardamom and white chocolate crunch

SET | PREP + COOK TIME **20 MINUTES + REFRIGERATION** | MAKES **32**

These addictive confections are perfect for serving as a treat after a meal, or wrapped and presented as a gift. The toasted macadamia nuts and pistachios, in tandem with the tart–sweet mixture of dried fruit, cut through the intense sweetness of the white chocolate.

1lb (450g) high-quality white chocolate, coarsely chopped

1 cup crisped rice cereal

1 cup golden raisins

1 cup macadamia nuts, toasted, coarsely chopped

1 cup finely chopped dried apricots

1 cup dried sweetened cranberries

3/4 cup pistachios, toasted, coarsely chopped

1 tsp ground cardamom

1 Grease a 9in x 13in (20cm x 30cm) rectangular cake pan. Line the bottom and the long sides with baking parchment, extending the parchment 2in (5cm) over the sides.

2 Melt the white chocolate in a large heatproof bowl over a large saucepan of simmering water (do not allow the water to touch the base of the bowl). Remove from the heat. Quickly stir in the remaining ingredients.

3 Press the mixture firmly into the prepared pan and smooth the top with a rubber spatula. Refrigerate for 2 hours or until firm. Cut into squares to serve.

Roast peach and star anise tart

BAKED | PREP + COOK TIME **1 HOUR 15 MINUTES** | SERVES **6**

This striking-looking tart has few ingredients but it's still a feast for the senses. You can use other fresh stone fruit, such as nectarines, plums, or apricots, in this recipe. Just remember to choose from the best seasonal produce available and use fruit that's just ripe.

2lb (900g) ripe small yellow peaches

1 vanilla bean (or 1 tsp vanilla extract)

2 tbsp butter, chopped

5 star anise pods

¼ cup sugar, plus extra 2 tbsp

1 sheet frozen pie dough, just thawed (see tips)

1¼ cups fresh soft ricotta cheese

1 Preheat the oven to 400°F (200°C). Grease a 9in (23cm) round pie dish.

2 Cut all but 2 of the peaches in half; remove the pits. Split the vanilla bean lengthwise, then cut in half crosswise. Put the peach halves, vanilla bean pieces, and chopped butter in a large bowl with the star anise and the ¼ cup sugar. Toss well to combine. Transfer to a roasting pan. Roast for 20 minutes or until the peaches are tender.

3 Meanwhile, ease the pie dough into the prepared pie dish. Prick the base all over with a fork. Cover. Refrigerate.

4 Remove the peaches from the roasting pan. Put the cooking juices, vanilla bean pieces, and star anise in a small saucepan. Bring to a boil. Cook for 5 minutes until reduced and syrupy. Set aside.

5 Place the pie dish on a baking sheet. Line the pie dough with parchment paper. Fill with dried beans or rice. Blind bake for 20 minutes. Remove the parchment and beans. Bake for 5 minutes longer or until pale golden.

6 Meanwhile, in a food processor, process the ricotta cheese and the extra 2 tablespoons sugar until combined.

7 Spread the ricotta mixture into the pie crust. Arrange the roasted peach halves on top. Bake the tart for 10 minutes or until the pastry is golden and the filling is heated through. Thinly slice the remaining 2 peaches.

8 Serve the tart topped with the slices of fresh peach and drizzled with the star anise syrup.

TIPS

• Depending on the brand, your frozen pie dough may be round instead of square. Still use 1 sheet.

• You can also make this tart in a round tart dish or a 6in x 10in (15cm x 25cm) loose-bottomed tart pan. For the rectangular pan, you'll need 2 sheets of pie dough and may need to trim it to fit.

• Before serving, sprinkle the tart with a small handful of roasted pistachios, hazelnuts, or pine nuts, if you like.

Spiced coconut rice pudding with saffron pears

STOVETOP | PREP + COOK TIME **1 HOUR** | SERVES **4**

Although this rice pudding can be served at room temperature, it's at its best when served immediately: fresh, fragrant, and warm. Choose just-ripe pears for this dish, as they will hold their shape and have a better texture after poaching.

³/₄ cup arborio rice

2 cups almond and coconut milk

¹/₂ cup coconut cream, plus extra ¹/₃ cup

¹/₄ cup sugar

2 fresh bay leaves

1 tsp salt

¹/₃ cup coconut flakes, toasted

saffron pears

¹/₂ cup sugar

¹/₂ tsp saffron threads (see tips)

2 star anise pods

3 green cardamom pods, bruised (see tips)

1 cinnamon stick

1lb (450g) ripe pears such as Anjou or Bartlett, peeled, halved, and cored (see tips)

1 To make the saffron pears, stir the sugar and 3 cups water in a medium saucepan over medium heat until the sugar dissolves. Bring to a simmer. Add the spices and pears, making sure the pears are fully immersed in the liquid. Reduce the heat to low. Poach the pears for 20 minutes or until tender; remove with a slotted spoon. Return the poaching liquid to the heat. Boil for 10 minutes or until the liquid has a syrupy consistency. Set aside to keep warm.

2 Meanwhile, to make the coconut rice, put the rice, the milk, the ¹/₂ cup of coconut cream, and the sugar in a deep nonstick medium saucepan over medium heat. Cook, stirring, until the mixture comes to a simmer. Stir in the bay leaves. Reduce the heat to low. Cook for 25 minutes or until the rice is just cooked. Stir in the salt.

3 Divide the rice pudding among 4 serving bowls. Top each serving with a little of the extra ¹/₃ cup coconut cream, a poached pear with some of the saffron syrup, and a sprinkling of the flaked coconut.

TIPS

- Instead of saffron, you can use ¹/₄ teaspoon ground turmeric, or a halved red beet to yield pinkish pears.
- To bruise the cardamom, strike the pods lightly with a rolling pin or pestle. Do not grind or break them. The seeds inside are edible. The pods are not.
- If the pears are very small, keep them whole and core them from the base using a melon baller.
- If you have time, you can poach the pears a day ahead. This will intensify the flavor and color.

Black pepper panna cotta with strawberry and basil granita

SET | PREP + COOK TIME **55 MINUTES + REFRIGERATION + FREEZING** | SERVES **6**

Pepper may not immediately spring to mind when you think of dessert, but it pairs beautifully with strawberries. It's used here in the creamy panna cotta. The panna cotta's warm, floral, and spicy notes complement the sweet acidity of the strawberry and basil granita.

$^3/_4$ cup fresh basil, plus extra to garnish

1 cup sugar, divided

8oz (225g) fresh strawberries, plus extra, sliced for serving (optional)

3 titanium-strength gelatin leaves (see tips)

1 cup milk

2$^1/_2$ cups heavy cream

2 tsp freshly ground black pepper (see tips)

1 To make the granita, put the $^3/_4$ cup basil in a small saucepan with $^3/_4$ cup of the sugar and 2$^1/_4$ cups water. Cook, stirring, over medium heat without boiling until the sugar dissolves. Bring to a simmer. Cook for 8 minutes. Let cool slightly.

2 Trim and hull the strawberries. Put them in a food processor. With the machine running, pour the syrup through a fine strainer over the strawberries. Discard any solids. Process until smooth and combined. Pour the mixture into a 9in x 9in (20cm x 30cm) baking dish or cake pan. Freeze the granita for 1 hour.

3 Using a fork, break up any ice crystals in the granita. Freeze for 3 hours longer, scraping with a fork every hour, until frozen.

4 Meanwhile, put the gelatin in a medium bowl of cold water. Soak for 5 minutes or until softened. Remove. Squeeze out any excess water. Set aside.

5 To make the panna cotta, put the milk, cream, remaining $^1/_4$ cup sugar, and black pepper in a medium saucepan over medium heat. Cook, stirring, until the sugar dissolves and the mixture is warm but not simmering. Remove the pan from the heat. Add the soaked gelatin and stir until dissolved. Strain the panna cotta mixture into a bowl. Cover the surface directly with plastic wrap. Refrigerate for 30 minutes.

6 Stir the panna cotta mixture. Pour into six $^3/_4$-cup serving glasses. Cover. Refrigerate for 3 hours or until set.

7 Top the panna cotta with the granita, the extra basil leaves, and extra sliced strawberries, if desired. Serve immediately.

TIPS

• Gelatin sheets come in different strengths (titanium, bronze, gold, and platinum.) Titanium works perfectly for panna cotta and is easy to find at your local specialty grocery.

• Use 2 teaspoons vanilla extract instead of the black pepper, if you like.

• The granita can be made a day ahead.

• Serve with shortbread cookies, almond cookies, or other ready-made cookies or wafers.

Panna cotta variations

With a name meaning "cooked cream" in Italian, panna cotta has a subtlety of flavor and a smooth, silky texture that make it perfect as a base for other, more dominant ingredients and flavor combinations, as in the recipes below.

Dark chocolate

Make the panna cotta mixture as described on page 134 but omitting the black pepper; reduce the cream to 1¼ cups and add an extra ½ cup milk. Chop 3.5oz (100g) dark chocolate (70% cocoa), reserving a few pieces for serving. Melt and stir into the panna cotta mixture until smooth. Continue with the recipe. Serve the panna cotta topped with extra pieces of dark chocolate.

Zesty lime

Make the panna cotta mixture as described on page 134, omitting the black pepper and adding 2 tablespoons finely grated lime zest to the cream mixture. After adding the gelatin, strain the mixture to remove the lime zest. Stir in 1 tablespoon lime juice. Continue with the recipe. Peel the zest thinly from 1 lime, avoiding the white pith; cut into long, thin strips. Serve the panna cotta drizzled with honey and topped with the strips of lime zest.

Raspberry and rose

Make the panna cotta mixture as described on page 134, omitting the black pepper. Purée 3.5oz (100g) thawed frozen raspberries. Push the purée through a fine strainer to remove any seeds. Add the strained purée to the panna cotta mixture with ½ teaspoon of rose water; stir well to combine. Continue with the recipe. Serve the panna cotta topped with extra raspberries and edible dried rose petals.

Eggnog

Make the panna cotta mixture as described on page 134, omitting the black pepper and adding ¼ teaspoon each of ground nutmeg and ground cinnamon to the cream mixture. Stir in 1 tablespoon of brandy. Continue with the recipe. Serve the panna cotta topped with a few pieces of cinnamon stick and a dusting of cinnamon and nutmeg.

Mandarin, honey, and coriander seed cake

BAKED | PREP + COOK TIME **1 HOUR 30 MINUTES** | SERVES **10**

While usually reserved for savory cooking, herbs actually work very well in sweet cooking.
The unique lemon-like flavor of coriander sweetened with sugar tickles the taste buds.
Its use here intensifies the distinctively floral notes of citrus and honey.

1½lb (700g) mandarin oranges (tangerines) or navel oranges

¼ cup coriander seeds

1 cup plus 4 tbsp butter, softened

⅔ cup sugar, plus extra ¾ cup

⅔ cup honey, plus extra ½ cup

4 eggs

1½ cups whole wheat flour

1 tsp baking soda

2 tsp baking powder

1 tsp salt

1½ cups hazelnut flour

1 cup sour cream

2 tbsp olive oil

1½ cups orange juice

3 sprigs lemon thyme

3 tsp orange blossom water

Greek yogurt, for serving

TIPS

• Mandarin oranges are popular for snacking because of their thin, easy-to-remove peels and lack of seeds. You'll need about 8 of them for this recipe.

• You could also serve the cake with extra heavy cream or labneh, if you like.

1 Place 2 mandarins or 1 navel orange in a small saucepan with enough water to cover. Bring to a boil over medium heat. Reduce the heat to low. Cook, covered, for 30 minutes or until soft. Drain. When cool enough to handle, open each orange with your fingers, remove any seeds, and add to a food processor. Process until smooth. Set aside.

2 Preheat the oven to 350°F (180°C). Grease a 9in (24cm) springform cake pan. Line the bottom with parchment paper.

3 Finely grate the zest from 2 of the remaining mandarins; you'll need 1 tablespoon zest. Use a zester to remove the zest from the remaining fruit in long, thin strips. Peel all the oranges, then cut into rounds. Put in a heatproof bowl.

4 Toast the coriander seeds in a small skillet over medium heat until fragrant. Crush, using a mortar and pestle or spice grinder. Reserve 2 tablespoons and set aside.

5 Using an electric mixer, beat the butter and ⅔ cup sugar until light and fluffy. Add the finely grated mandarin zest, coriander, and the ⅔ cup of honey. Beat until well combined. Add the eggs, one at a time, beating well between additions. Fold in the flour, baking soda, baking powder, salt, and hazelnut flour, then the sour cream, olive oil, and mandarin purée in 2 batches. Pour the mixture into the prepared cake pan. Smooth the surface. Bake for 1 hour, covering with foil if over-browning, or until a toothpick inserted into the cake's center comes out clean. Leave in pan.

6 Meanwhile, combine the orange juice, extra ¾ cup sugar, extra ½ cup honey, thyme, strips of zest, and reserved coriander in a medium saucepan. Stir over medium heat until the sugar is dissolved. Simmer for 5 minutes; stir in the orange blossom water. Prick the cake all over with a fine skewer. Pour 1 cup of the hot syrup over the cake. Pour the rest over the mandarin slices. Let cool. Serve the cake with the sliced mandarins in syrup and the yogurt.

Ginger, rhubarb, and pear lattice tart

BAKED | PREP + COOK TIME **1 HOUR 40 MINUTES + REFRIGERATION, FREEZING + COOLING** | SERVES **12**

Weaving a classic pastry lattice on top of this tart creates an impressive visual appeal, especially with the ruby-red fruit filling peeking out from below. It is not as difficult to do as it looks, though. Under-and-over repetition is the key action.

4$^1/_3$ cups flour

1 cup sugar

1$^1/_2$ cups (3 sticks) cold butter, chopped, plus extra for greasing

2 egg yolks

2 tbsp chilled water

1 egg, lightly beaten

$^1/_4$ cup demerara sugar

rhubarb and pear filling

1$^1/_2$ lb (750g) trimmed rhubarb stalks, chopped

2 pears, peeled, cut into $^3/_4$ in (2cm) pieces

$^1/_3$ cup sugar

$^1/_4$ cup crystallized ginger, chopped

1$^1/_2$ tsp vanilla extract

TIPS

• The rhubarb and pear filling can be made up to 2 days ahead. Refrigerate in an airtight container until needed.

• The pie dough can be made 1 day ahead. Wrap the portions in plastic wrap and refrigerate.

• After baking, allow the tart to cool completely before removing it from the pan.

1 Preheat the oven to 350°F (180°C). Grease a loose-bottomed fluted tart pan that's 2in (5cm) deep with a top measurement of 10½in (26.5cm) and a base measurement of 9in (23cm).

2 To make the filling, put the rhubarb, pears, and sugar in a baking dish. Roast for 30 minutes. Transfer to a medium saucepan. Cook, stirring, over high heat for 5 minutes or until thick. Let cool. Stir in the ginger and vanilla. Cover; refrigerate until needed.

3 In a food processor, pulse the flour, sugar, and butter until the mixture resembles coarse crumbs. Add the egg yolks and chilled water. Pulse until the dough just comes together. Do not overmix. Knead gently on a lightly floured surface. Divide into two-third and one-third portions. Form each into a disc. Wrap in plastic wrap. Refrigerate for 30 minutes.

4 Roll out the larger portion of dough between sheets of parchment paper until $^1/_8$ in (3mm) thick. Lift it into the tart pan. Ease it into the sides; trim edges. Prick the bottom all over with a fork. Cover. Freeze for 10 minutes.

5 Place tart pan on a baking sheet. Line pie dough with parchment paper, then fill with dried beans or rice. Bake for 20 minutes or until edges are crisp and base is half-cooked. Carefully remove the paper and beans. Bake for 10 minutes longer until crust is golden and crisp. Let cool.

6 Roll out the remaining dough between sheets of parchment paper into a 10in x 14in (25cm x 35cm) rectangle. Use a ruler and a sharp knife to cut 12 pastry strips that each measure $^3/_4$ in x 10in (2cm x 25cm). Slide the parchment with the strips onto a tray. Cover; refrigerate until needed.

7 Spoon the filling into the pie crust. Lightly brush the crust's edge with a little beaten egg. Place pastry strips on top of the filling, weaving as you go, to form a lattice; trim the ends. Brush with a little more egg; sprinkle with demerara sugar. Place tart on baking sheet. Bake on the top shelf of the oven for 25 minutes or until crust is golden and crisp. Let cool on baking sheet for 20 minutes; transfer to a wire rack to cool completely.

Coconut, makrut lime, and pineapple syrup cake

BAKED | PREP + COOK TIME **1 HOUR 15 MINUTES + STANDING + COOLING** | SERVES **8**

The makrut lime is grown for its distinctive double leaves rather than its fruit. The leaves are quite different in scent and flavor from ordinary lime leaves. They taste fresh, strong, and somewhat sweet. They're rather tough, so they're usually shredded very finely prior to use.

2 fresh makrut lime leaves (see tips)

1 cup sugar, divided

½ cup plus 3 tbsp butter, softened, plus extra for greasing

3 eggs

½ cup sour cream

1¾ cups flour

1 tsp baking soda

1 tsp baking powder

½ tsp salt

1 cup flaked coconut

1lb (450g) fresh pineapple, sliced thinly

toasted shredded coconut, to garnish

lime cheeks, for serving (optional)

makrut lime syrup

8 large fresh makrut lime leaves

1⅓ cups sugar

⅔ cup lime juice

TIPS

- You can find makrut lime leaves at your favorite Asian grocery.
- Remove the tough center rib of the lime leaves before shredding.
- Store the cake in an airtight container for up to 3 days, or refrigerate for up to 5 days. Warm gently before serving to refresh.

1 Preheat the oven to 325°F (160°C). Grease a 5in x 9 in (12cm x 23cm) loaf pan. Line the bottom and long sides with parchment paper, extending the paper 2in (5cm) over the sides.

2 Remove the makrut lime leaves from the stems; discard the stems. Put the leaves and ¼ cup of the sugar in a small food processor: process until very finely ground.

3 Using an electric mixer, beat the butter, lime-leaf sugar, and remaining sugar in a large bowl until light and fluffy. Beat in the eggs, one at a time, then the sour cream. Stir in the flour, baking soda, baking powder, salt, and coconut. Spoon the mixture into the prepared pan. Smooth the surface.

4 Bake the cake for 50–55 minutes or until a toothpick inserted into the center comes out clean. Leave the cake in the pan for 5 minutes before turning out, top-side up, onto a wire rack set over a baking sheet.

5 Meanwhile, make the makrut lime syrup. Coarsely tear half of the lime leaves. Put the torn leaves, sugar, lime juice, and 1 cup water in a small saucepan over low heat. Stir, without boiling, until the sugar dissolves. Bring to a boil. Remove from the heat. Let stand for 5 minutes; discard the torn lime leaves. Finely shred the remaining lime leaves (see the second tip). Stir into the hot syrup.

6 Poke the top of cake lightly all over with a fork. Pour half the hot syrup evenly over the top and side of the hot cake. Let cool.

7 Put the pineapple in a medium bowl. Pour the remaining hot syrup over it. Set aside to cool.

8 Serve the cake with the pineapple in syrup, sprinkled with toasted shredded coconut, and with lime cheeks for squeezing over, if you like.

Little ginger citrus cakes

BAKED | PREP + COOK TIME **50 MINUTES + COOLING** | SERVES **12**

These little spiced cakes are a great choice for a luncheon or tea party. They're such a pretty picture that it's almost a shame to eat them—almost. Drizzled with a simple lemon icing, they yield a sublime punch of warm, vibrant, citrusy flavor in a small but perfect package.

2 tbsp butter, melted

³/₄ cup flour

³/₄ tsp baking soda

¹/₂ tsp baking powder

¹/₂ tsp salt

³/₄ cup almond flour

³/₄ cup sugar

¹/₃ cup extra virgin olive oil

2 eggs, lightly beaten

¹/₃ cup freshly squeezed orange juice, strained

3 tsp finely grated lemon zest

2 tsp ground ginger

1 tsp fresh thyme leaves, minced

1 tbsp loosely packed fresh thyme tips, to garnish

lemon icing

1¹/₄ cups powdered sugar

about ¹/₄ cup lemon juice, strained

1. Preheat the oven to 350°F (180°C). Using with the melted butter, grease and flour a 12-hole 3in (7cm) (¹/₂-cup [125ml]) mini fluted tube pan. Tap any excess flour out of the pan.

2. Sift the flour, baking soda, baking powder, and salt into a large bowl. Whisk in the almond flour and sugar. Add the olive oil, eggs, orange juice, lemon zest, ground ginger, and thyme leaves until just combined. Spoon the mixture into the prepared holes of the mini tube pan .

3. Bake the cakes for 20 minutes or until a toothpick inserted into the center comes out clean. To prevent the cakes from sticking to the pan, upon removing the pan from the oven immediately place it right-side up on a wire rack with a damp, clean kitchen towel resting over the top. The steam this creates increases the chances of the cakes releasing from the sides of the pan. After 5 minutes have passed, run a knife around the outside and inner edges of the cakes, then turn them out onto a wire rack to cool.

4. Meanwhile, make the lemon icing. Sift the powdered sugar into a medium bowl. Stir in enough of the lemon juice to form an icing the consistency of honey (be careful not to add too much lemon juice, as it combines with the powdered sugar fairly quickly). Drizzle the icing over the cakes, and top with the fresh thyme tips.

TIP

You can instead use a large fluted tube pan to make one cake. Simply increase the baking time to 35–40 minutes.

Orange and rosemary labneh tart

BAKED | PREP + COOK TIME **1 HOUR 30 MINUTES + REFRIGERATION + COOLING** | SERVES **8**

Sweet and tangy from the home-made labneh, this simple baked cheesecake is remarkably easy to put together, even allowing for the overnight draining time. A creamy, light-textured filling infused with the flavors of honey and rosemary is the worthy result.

You will need to start this recipe the day before

3 cups Greek yogurt

3 eggs

2 tbsp honey

1 tsp vanilla extract

2 tsp finely chopped fresh rosemary leaves

2 cups apple juice

a sprig of rosemary, plus extra tips, to garnish

1¼ lb (600g) navel oranges, thinly sliced

shortcrust pastry

1½ cups flour

2 tbsp powdered sugar

½ cup plus 4 tbsp cold butter, chopped

2 tbsp iced water

TIP

To make a glaze for the top of the tart, simmer 1 cup of the orange poaching liquid with ¼ cup honey over medium heat until the mixture is reduced by half and syrupy.

1 To make the labneh, line a strainer with a piece of cheesecloth. Place the strainer over a large bowl. Spoon the yogurt into the cheese cloth, cover the bowl, and refrigerate overnight.

2 The next day, to make the shortcrust pastry, in a food processor pulse the flour, sugar, and butter until the mixture resembles breadcrumbs. Add the iced water; process until the dough just comes together. Shape into a disc. Wrap in plastic wrap; refrigerate for 30 minutes.

3 Grease a 4½in x 14in (11cm x 34cm) loose-bottomed rectangular fluted tart pan. Roll out the pie dough on a floured surface or between sheets of parchment paper until large enough to line the pan. Lift the pie dough into the tart pan; press over the bottom and sides. Trim away excess pastry. Prick the bottom of the pie dough all over with a fork. Refrigerate for 30 minutes.

4 Preheat the oven to 400°F (200°C).

5 Place the tart pan on a baking sheet. Line the pie dough with parchment paper; fill with dried beans or rice. Bake for 10 minutes. Remove the parchment and beans. Bake for 10 minutes longer or until lightly browned. Let cool. Reduce the oven temperature to 275°F (140°C).

6 Whisk together the labneh, eggs, honey, vanilla, and chopped rosemary. Spoon the mixture into the cooled pie crust. Bake 25 minutes or until just set. Let cool to room temperature. Refrigerate the tart until cold.

7 Meanwhile, put the apple juice and sprig of rosemary in a medium saucepan. Bring to a boil over medium heat. Add the orange slices; reduce the heat to low. Simmer for 15 minutes until tender. Let cool.

8 Just before serving, drain the orange slices and arrange over the tart. Top with the extra rosemary tips.

Crostoli with vanilla custard cream

FRIED | PREP + COOK TIME **1 HOUR + STANDING + REFRIGERATION** | SERVES **6**

Crostoli are crisp fried pastries consisting of ribbons of dough fried and dusted with sugar. They're traditionally served at Carnevale. Known by various names across Italy, with several regional variations, they are a bite-sized morsel of deliciousness whatever they're called.

1¼ cups flour

½ tsp baking powder

½ tsp salt

1½ tbsp powdered sugar, plus extra, sifted, to dust

1 tsp vanilla extract

2 tsp olive oil

1 egg

about 1 tbsp marsala wine or sweet sherry

vegetable oil for deep-frying

8oz (225g) fresh strawberries, halved, for serving

vanilla custard cream

2 cups milk

$^2/_3$ cup sugar

4 egg yolks

$^1/_3$ cup flour

$^2/_3$ cup heavy cream

2 tsp vanilla extract

TIPS

- Crostoli chips can be made a day ahead, then stored in an airtight container. Dust them with powdered sugar just before serving.
- Flavor the custard with orange liqueur, grated orange rind, or finely chopped chocolate, if you like.
- The custard can be made a day ahead. Store it in the fridge until needed.

1 Make the vanilla custard cream. Warm the milk in a medium saucepan over medium heat until just below boiling. Whisk together the sugar, egg yolks, and flour in a small bowl until smooth. Whisk the hot milk into the egg yolk mixture. Return the mixture to the same pan. Cook over low heat, whisking continuously, for 5 minutes or until the mixture boils and thickens. Remove from the heat. Cover the surface of the custard directly with plastic wrap. Let cool for 15 minutes. Refrigerate for 30 minutes. Using an electric mixer, beat the cream and vanilla in a small bowl until soft peaks form. Whisk the cream into the chilled custard until smooth.

2 To make the crostoli, put the flour, baking powder, salt, and the 1½ tablespoons powdered sugar in a food processor. Process to combine. Add the vanilla, olive oil, egg, and just enough of the marsala wine to make the ingredients come together. Knead the dough on a floured work surface until smooth. Wrap in plastic wrap. Let stand at room temperature for 30 minutes.

3 Cut the dough in half. Working with one piece at a time, lightly flour the dough, pressing with the palm of your hand to flatten slightly. Place on a lightly floured work surface. Using a sheet of parchment paper and a rolling pin, roll the dough out to a thickness of $^1/_8$in (3mm). Use a crinkle-edge ravioli cutter to cut the dough into 2in x 5in (5cm x 12cm) strips. Make 2 small slits in the center of each strip.

4 Heat just enough vegetable oil for deep-frying in a large saucepan over medium heat until it reaches 350°F (180°C). Cook the dough strips, in batches, for 15 seconds on each side or until light golden and crisp. Drain on paper towels. Let cool.

5 Dust the crostoli with the extra sifted powdered sugar. Serve with the strawberries and vanilla custard cream.

Sweet polenta with rhubarb and sweet dukkah

BAKED AND STOVETOP | PREP + COOK TIME **35 MINUTES** | SERVES **4**

Traditionally savory Egyptian dukkah gets a sweet makeover in this delightful dessert of creamy polenta and roasted rhubarb. The crunch and aroma of the nuts, seeds, and spices in the dukkah provide a counterpoint to the tart-sweet rhubarb.

10oz (300g) trimmed rhubarb

2¹/₂ cups milk

¹/₂ cup coconut milk

¹/₄ cup honey

²/₃ cup white polenta

sweet dukkah

1¹/₂ tbsp unsalted hazelnuts

1¹/₂ tbsp pistachios

1 tbsp sesame seeds

3 tsp coriander seeds

2¹/₂ tsp light brown sugar

³/₄ tsp ground cinnamon

³/₄ tsp ground cardamom

1 Preheat the oven to 400°F (200°C). Line a baking sheet with parchment paper.

2 Cut the rhubarb into 4in (10cm) lengths. Place in a baking dish and cover with foil. Roast for 20 minutes (see tips) or until the rhubarb is soft but still holds its shape. Carefully transfer to a plate, leaving one piece of rhubarb behind in the pan. Leave the oven on.

3 Add 2 tablespoons water to the rhubarb in the pan. Mash until the mixture breaks up. Cook over medium-low heat, stirring, for 1 minute or until the rhubarb breaks down into the consistency of sauce. Remove from the heat. Cover to keep warm.

4 Make the sweet dukkah. Put the nuts and seeds on the baking sheet. Roast for 5 minutes. Coarsely crush using a mortar and pestle. Let cool. Put the sugar, cinnamon, and cardamom in a small bowl; add the nut mixture. Mix well.

5 Meanwhile, whisk together the milk, coconut milk, honey, and 1 cup of water in a medium saucepan. Bring to a boil. Reduce the heat to low. Slowly pour the polenta into the pan. Cook, whisking constantly, for 2 minutes or until thick.

6 Divide the polenta evenly among 4 serving bowls. Top evenly with the rhubarb and rhubarb sauce. Sprinkle with the dukkah to serve.

TIPS

- The cooking time for the rhubarb may vary according to thickness and ripeness, so check after 15 minutes; continue to cook only if needed.
- The rhubarb can be cooked the day before. Store it in the fridge, in an airtight container large enough that the rhubarb holds its shape.

Blueberry basil ice cream pops

FROZEN | PREP + COOK TIME **50 MINUTES + COOLING, REFRIGERATION + FREEZING** | MAKES **12**

These creamy frozen pops are particularly cooling and refreshing on a hot summer day, and the rich purple swirls of blueberry are hard to resist. Although you do need to allow time for cooling and freezing, this is a no-churn ice cream so it cuts down on fuss factor.

You will need 12 wooden craft sticks for this recipe

8oz (225g) blueberries (see tips)

1½ cups firmly packed basil leaves, shredded (see tips)

1 cup heavy cream

1 cup milk

4 egg yolks

½ cup pure maple syrup

1½ cups Greek yogurt

TIPS

• Use fresh rather than frozen blueberries for this recipe because they give the best color and flavor to the finished ice cream pops.

• For a different flavor combination, swap the blueberries and basil with raspberries and mint.

• Trim a quarter length off the ends of the craft sticks so they are not too long. Or, if you like, omit them. Simply set the ice cream in the loaf pan, then scoop to serve.

• If you're not serving the ice cream pops immediately, return the pops to the freezer, individually wrapped in freezer paper.

1 Put the blueberries and ¼ cup water in a small saucepan. Cook, covered, over medium heat for 4 minutes or until the blueberries release their juices and collapse. Remove the lid. Cook for 4 minutes longer or until thick and syrupy. Remove from the heat. Stir in the basil. Let stand until cooled to room temperature.

2 Put the cream and milk in a small heavy-based saucepan; bring to a simmer over medium-low heat. Do not boil.

3 Using a food processor or blender, purée the cooled blueberry mixture. Push it through a fine-mesh strainer over a bowl. Discard the solids.

4 In a large bowl, whisk the egg yolks and maple syrup until thick and pale. Add the warm milk mixture in a thin stream, whisking constantly until combined. Return the mixture to the saucepan over medium heat. Cook, stirring constantly (you may need to move the pan slightly off the heat to ensure the mixture doesn't boil during this time) for 10 minutes or until it thickens and coats the back of a wooden spoon. Remove from the heat.

5 Put the yogurt in a medium heatproof bowl. Whisk in the egg-and-milk mixture until combined. Refrigerate for 30 minutes or until chilled.

6 Line a 6-cup (1.5l) loaf pan with parchment paper, extending the parchment ¾in (2cm) above the edges of the pan. Pour in the chilled yogurt mixture. Drizzle over the blueberry mixture. Using a spatula, gently swirl the blueberry mixture to create a marbled effect. Freeze for 2 hours until the mixture is partially set. Cover the pan firmly with foil. Using the tip of a small, sharp knife, make 12 small, evenly spaced cuts in the foil. Insert the craft sticks through the cuts and into the ice cream. Freeze for 4 hours longer or overnight until firm.

7 To serve, let the ice cream stand at room temperature for 5 minutes to soften slightly, then remove from the pan. Use a hot, dry serrated knife to cut the ice cream into 12 even-sized servings. Serve immediately.

Pecan and pear spiced soufflé cake

BAKED | PREP + COOK TIME **1 HOUR 20 MINUTES + COOLING** | SERVES **10**

This is a lovely cake for a special occasion, or when having family and friends around for lunch or dinner. Pears add an elegant touch to a dessert, particularly firm varieties that hold their shape but intensify in sweetness on cooking.

1lb (450g) Bosc pears, halved lengthwise

$^2/_3$ cup pecans, divided

4 large eggs

$^1/_4$ cup honey

1 tsp vanilla extract

$^3/_4$ tsp ground nutmeg

$^1/_2$ tsp ground cinnamon

$^1/_4$ tsp ground cloves

2 tbsp whole wheat flour

1 tbsp corn starch

$^1/_4$ tsp salt

3 tbsp butter, melted, cooled, plus extra for greasing

$^1/_3$ cup Greek yogurt

1 Preheat the oven to 350°F (180°C). Line two baking sheets with parchment paper. Grease and line the bottom of a 9in (22cm) springform cake pan with parchment paper.

2 Place the pears, skin-side up, on one of the baking sheets. Roast for 40 minutes. Meanwhile, place the pecans on another baking sheet. Roast on another oven shelf for the last 5 minutes of the pear roasting time. Let cool.

3 Process $^1/_2$ cup of the pecans until finely ground. Coarsely chop the remaining pecans; reserve. Cut each pear half into 5 wedges (to make 20 wedges in total). Core, if you like.

4 Using an electric mixer, whip the eggs, honey, vanilla, nutmeg, cinnamon, and cloves for 10 minutes or until ribbons form when the beaters are lifted. Sift the whole wheat flour, cornstarch, and salt over the egg mixture. Add the ground pecans and melted butter. Using a large whisk, gently incorporate the ingredients into the mixture.

5 Pour the mixture into the prepared cake pan. Bake the cake on the lower shelf of the oven for 20 minutes. Let cool in the pan for 10 minutes before removing the collar of the pan. The cake will collapse as it cools.

6 Cut the cake into 10 equal slices. Sprinkle with the reserved pecans. Serve 1 cake slice and 2 pear wedges per person, with a drizzle of yogurt over the top.

TIP

This cake is best made on the day of serving.

SPECIAL OCCASIONS

These are desserts that stand out. From dinner parties and casual entertaining to festive celebrations that mark a special day, you can match the dish to the moment.

Chocolate hazelnut ice cream pandoro

FROZEN | PREP + COOK TIME **25 MINUTES + FREEZING + STANDING** | SERVES **10**

Pandoro, a sweet Italian yeast bread with a long history, is traditionally prepared and served around Christmas and New Year, much like panettone. It is usually cooked in a special pandoro pan that gives the bread its majestic conical star shape.

You will need to start this recipe a day ahead

1lb (500g) purchased pandoro cake (see tips)

1 cup chocolate-hazelnut spread

1/4 cup raspberry jam

1 quart (4 cups/1l) salted caramel ice cream (see tips)

1/4 cup powdered sugar, sifted

8oz (225g) raspberries, to garnish

high-quality thick vanilla custard, for serving, optional

1 Freeze the pandoro for at least 2 hours or until firm.

2 Turn the pandoro upside down on a cutting board. Using a long, thin sharp knife, held at an angle, cut out a 4in (12cm) circle from the base of the pandoro. It should have the shape of a wide but shallow cone. Trim off the tip of the cone, leaving a flat disk about 1in (2.5cm) thick. Reserve the disk; you'll replace it after you fill the pandoro. Continue to hollow out the pandoro as neatly as possible, leaving a 1in (2.5cm) wall all around. Remove the center pieces. Because the pandoro is star-shaped, it will be thinner in some parts and thicker in others. Reserve the pandoro offcuts for another use (see tips).

3 Use a small spatula to spread the chocolate-hazelnut spread over the inside of the pandoro. Spoon the raspberry jam into the bottom. Freeze for 30 minutes.

4 Meanwhile, remove the ice cream from the freezer. Let it soften for 15 minutes.

5 Spoon the ice cream into the center of the pandoro, a little at a time. Replace the reserved pandoro disk. Cover. Freeze for 4 hours or overnight until firm. Remove the pandoro from the freezer 15 minutes before serving.

6 Dust the pandoro with the sifted powdered sugar, garnish with the raspberries, and serve with the custard, if you like.

TIPS

- Pandoro is an Italian cake available during the holidays. Purchase one from your favorite specialty grocery store or order it online.
- If pandoro is unavailable, use panettone; your dessert won't have the same star shape, however.
- Use the pandoro offcuts to make trifles, Christmas truffles, or bread and butter pudding.
- We used a salted caramel ice cream with chocolate-coated hazelnuts. You can use your favorite flavor.

Raspberry and almond trifle

SET | PREP + COOK TIME **35 MINUTES + COOLING + REFRIGERATION** | SERVES **10**

Trifle is a real crowd-pleaser at special occasions or when you're gathered around the table for lunch with family or friends, and any leftovers never seem to go uneaten. Take advantage of the most luscious seasonal berries available to make this traditional classic.

2 x 6oz (170g) boxes of raspberry- or strawberry-flavored gelatin

16oz (450g) fresh strawberries, divided

8oz (225g) raspberries, divided

8oz (225g) purchased sponge cake or butter cake, cut into 1¼ in (3cm) cubes (see tips)

⅓ cup sweet sherry, such as Pedro Ximénez (see tips)

2 cups mascarpone

4 cups pre-made vanilla pudding (see tips)

2¼ cups heavy cream

2 tbsp powdered sugar, divided

2 tbsp flaked almonds

1 Make the gelatin according to the package instructions. Pour into a 12-cup (3l) glass serving bowl. Cut 8oz (250g) of the strawberries in half. Add to the unset jelly with half of the raspberries. Refrigerate for 1 hour or until almost set.

2 Put the cubes of cake in a medium bowl; sprinkle with the sherry. Toss to coat.

3 Using an electric mixer, beat the mascarpone and pudding in a large bowl until soft peaks form. Spoon the mixture over the gelatin. Top with the sherry-soaked cake.

4 Beat the heavy cream and 1 tablespoon of the sifted powdered sugar in a large bowl using an electric mixer until soft peaks form. Spoon the cream over the cake.

5 Serve the trifle topped with the remaining berries and the flaked almonds. Dust with the remaining 1 tablespoon sifted powdered sugar.

TIPS

- If making your own butter cake, you can use the recipe on page 104 for Spanish caramel orange cake. Halve the quantity and work through step 3. Or use your favorite sponge cake recipe instead.
- You can use orange juice or orange-flavored liqueur instead of the sherry, if you like.
- You can use cooked vanilla pudding, if you'd like. You'll need 2 x 3.4oz (96g) boxes to make 4 cups.
- The trifle can be made 1 day ahead, up to the end of step 3. Store, covered, in the fridge.

Fruit cake ice cream bombes

FROZEN | PREP + COOK TIME **30 MINUTES + STANDING + FREEZING** | SERVES **8**

Wondering what to do with that fruitcake or Christmas pudding someone sent you as a gift? Here's a recipe that transforms it into a dessert elegant enough for any festive table. Whether made in individual portions or as one large show-stopper, this dessert is easy and impressive.

You will need to start this recipe the day before

butter for greasing

10oz (300g) dark fruit cake, spiced gingerbread, or Christmas pudding, coarsely chopped

2 tbsp liqueur of your choice (see tips)

2 quarts (8 cups/2l) vanilla ice cream, softened slightly

1 cup pecans, toasted, coarsely chopped

orange slices

1lb (450g) navel oranges

$^1/_4$ cup honey, plus extra, for serving (optional)

1. Grease eight 1-cup (250ml) ramekins or molds (see tips).

2. Combine the cake and liqueur in a large bowl until the liqueur is absorbed. Working quickly, add the ice cream to the bowl, and then the pecans. Stir until just combined. Spoon the ice cream mixture into the prepared molds. Freeze for 4 hours or overnight until firm.

3. To make the orange slices, preheat the oven to 325°F (160°C). Line a large baking sheet with parchment paper. Cut the oranges into $^3/_{16}$ in (4mm) thick slices. Brush the slices with honey. Arrange the slices, in a single layer, on the lined baking sheet. Bake for 45 minutes or until they start to caramelize. Leave on the baking sheet to cool.

4. Just before serving, turn out the bombes onto chilled plates or a platter. Top with the orange slices and extra honey, if you like. Serve immediately.

TIPS

- You can use brandy or an orange, coffee, nut, or vanilla liqueur.
- You can use any sort of mold for this dessert, from fluted glasses to plastic cups. Ramekins, individual pie pans, or even large wine goblets will do, as long as they hold about 1 cup.
- For a large bombe, line an 8-cup (2l) mold or bowl with 2 large pieces of plastic wrap, extending the plastic 4in (10cm) over the side.
- The orange slices can be made 1 day ahead. Store in an airtight container at room temperature, layered with baking parchment to prevent the slices from sticking together.

Eton mess wreath

ASSEMBLED | PREP + COOK TIME **30 MINUTES + STANDING** | SERVES **6**

The origin story has it that a dessert dropped at a sporting event at the British school Eton was scooped off the floor and served in bowls anyway, despite being a smashed mess—hence this dessert's name. This concoction of meringues and fruit looks as good as it tastes.

8 oz (225g) fresh raspberries, divided

1 tbsp powdered sugar, plus extra, sifted, to dust (optional)

1³/₄ cup white chocolate baking chips

6 coconut macarons

4 raspberry macarons

4 strawberry macarons

8oz (225g) fresh strawberries, halved

8oz (225g) fresh cherries

4 small plain meringue cookies

unsprayed edible flowers, to garnish (optional)

2 cups whipped cream, for serving

1 Reserve ²/₃ cup of the raspberries. Process the remaining 1 cup of raspberries and the powdered sugar until puréed. Push the purée through a fine strainer over a small bowl. Cover; refrigerate until needed.

2 Place 2 sheets of parchment paper, slightly overlapping, on the counter to create a wider sheet. Using a 12in (30cm) bowl, trace a circle. Using a second 8in (20cm) bowl, trace a second circle in the center of the first one. You now have a template for the white chocolate ring.

3 Stir the chocolate in a heatproof bowl over a saucepan of gently simmering water until melted (don't allow the base of the bowl to touch the water). Using the template as a guide, drop spoonfuls of chocolate inside the borders of the ring; using the back of a spoon, spread the chocolate thickly and evenly to fill the ring. Let stand until set.

4 Carefully transfer the chocolate ring to a large serving board or flat platter. Arrange the macarons evenly around the ring, then scatter the strawberries, cherries (pitted and halved, if you prefer), and remaining ²/₃ cup raspberries between them.

5 Crush the meringues over the wreath. Sprinkle the flowers over the wreath, if using. Dust with a little extra powdered sugar and drizzle with a little of the raspberry sauce.

6 Serve the wreath with the remaining raspberry sauce and whipped cream in separate bowls.

No-churn almond and honey parfait

FROZEN | PREP + COOK TIME **40 MINUTES + COOLING, FREEZING + STANDING** | SERVES **8**

In France, parfaits are frozen desserts made of airy whipped custards and creams. For this beautiful dessert, you can choose individual cups or a terrine mold to give diners a gorgeous slice filled with a glorious melding of smooth creaminess, nutty crunch, and fragrant honey.

You will need to start this recipe a day ahead

14oz (400g) fresh ricotta cheese

2 tsp vanilla extract

$2/3$ cup honey, plus extra, to serve

2 cups Greek yogurt

$1/2$ cup toasted almonds, coarsely chopped, plus extra, to garnish

1   Line the bottom of a 4in x 9$1/4$in (10.5cm x 23.5cm) terrine mold or loaf pan with parchment paper, extending the paper over the two long sides.

2   In a food processor, combine the ricotta cheese, vanilla, honey, and yogurt until smooth. Transfer the mixture to a large bowl. Fold in the chopped almonds. Spoon the mixture into the prepared mold or pan. Smooth the top. Cover tightly with plastic wrap, then foil.

3   Freeze for 8 hours or overnight until firm.

4   Wipe the outside of the pan with a warm cloth. Using the long sides of parchment paper, carefully lift the parfait out of the mold and transfer it to a platter. Drizzle with extra honey and sprinkle with chopped almonds. Cut the parfait into slices to serve.

No-churn parfait variations

The beauty of a frozen dessert is that it can be made well in advance and brought to the table with a minimum of stress. Use any of these clever parfait variations to bring a refreshing restaurant-quality dish to your dinner party or family celebration.

Smashed blackberry and halva

Make the no-churn parfait as described on page 166, omitting the almonds. Fold in $1/2$ cup pistachios, 8oz (225g) thawed, mashed frozen blackberries, and 3.5oz (100g) crumbled chocolate-swirled halva. Continue with the recipe. Serve the parfait drizzled with $1/2$ cup blackberry jam warmed with 2 tablespoons water, and then topped with extra fresh blackberries.

Lemon curd and shortbread

Make the no-churn parfait as described on page 166, omitting the almonds. Chop 8oz (225g) all-butter shortbread cookies into small pieces. Place in a strainer and shake out any small loose crumbs. Fold the cookie pieces into the parfait mixture. Stir a 10oz (300g) jar of lemon curd until it becomes smooth. Add the lemon curd to the parfait mixture and fold it through to partially combine. Continue with the recipe. Serve the parfait with thin slices of lemon.

Berries and chocolate

Make the no-churn parfait as described on page 166, omitting the almonds. Stir in $1/2$ cup toasted hazelnuts, 3.5oz (100g) chopped dark chocolate (70% cocoa), 3.5oz (100g) fresh or frozen raspberries, and 3.5oz (100g) fresh or frozen halved pitted cherries. Continue with the recipe. Serve with extra raspberries and toasted hazelnuts.

Black sesame and coconut

Make the no-churn parfait as described on page 166, omitting the almonds. Stir in 2 teaspoons sesame oil. Combine with $1/2$ cup (35g) toasted shredded coconut and 1 tablespoon black sesame seeds. Continue with the recipe. Serve the parfait topped with lychees in syrup, lime slices, and strips of lime zest.

Burnt Basque cheesecake

BAKED | PREP + COOK TIME **1 HOUR 5 MINUTES** | SERVES **8**

This crustless cheesecake originated in San Sebastian, part of Spain's Basque region, in the 1990s. The high temperature at which it is cooked creates a "burnt" caramelized crust around the outside, protecting the interior and as a result keeping it soft, creamy, and light.

16oz (550g) cream cheese, room temperature

³/₄ cup sugar

3 eggs, room temperature

1 cup heavy cream, room temperature, plus extra, chilled, to serve

¹/₂ tsp salt

1 tsp vanilla extract

2 tbsp flour

1 Preheat the oven to 400°F (200°C). Butter the bottom and sides of a 9in (23cm) springform cake pan. Line the bottom with parchment paper.

2 Using an electric mixer fitted with a paddle attachment, beat the cream cheese until very smooth. Add the sugar. Beat for 2 minutes or until the sugar is dissolved. Add the eggs, one at a time, beating well between additions. Add the 1 cup of heavy cream, salt, and vanilla. Beat until just combined. Sift the flour over the mixture. Beat on low speed until combined, then on medium speed for 10 seconds or just until smooth. Pour the mixture into the lined pan.

3 Bake the cheesecake for about 50-60 minutes until dark on top but still wobbly in the center. Remove from the oven. Let cool completely in the pan; the cheesecake will sink upon cooling.

4 Serve cut into wedges, with extra heavy cream for dolloping over the top.

TIPS

• Preheating the oven to the right temperature is important; it needs to be hot before the cheesecake goes in, so that the crust caramelizes properly.

• Make sure the cream cheese, eggs, and cream are all at room temperature before combining them; this helps them to blend smoothly.

• This cheesecake is best made on the day of serving, but will keep in an airtight container in the fridge for up to 3 days. Bring to room temperature before serving.

Vincotto crème caramel with cherries

BAKED | PREP + COOK TIME **1 HOUR 20 MINUTES + REFRIGERATION** | SERVES **12**

Vincotto is a syrupy sweet-flavored vinegar you may never have come across, but when combined with crème caramel it makes for a sophisticated sauce. You may find it in cherry or blueberry flavors, or you can create your own with equal parts fig vinegar and balsamic glaze.

1 cup sugar

¹/₄ cup vincotto

6 eggs

1¹/₄ cups milk

1 x 14oz (396g) can sweetened condensed milk

fresh cherries, to serve (see tips)

1 Lightly grease a 9in x9in (23cm x 23cm) baking dish. Place it in a larger roasting pan lined with a kitchen towel. The roasting pan should be deep enough to allow water to come halfway up the sides of the baking dish.

2 Put the sugar and 2 tablespoons water in a small saucepan over medium heat. Stir until the sugar dissolves. Bring to a boil, without stirring. Boil for 8 minutes or until golden brown. Carefully pour in the vincotto. Boil for 1 minute longer. Pour the caramel into the prepared baking dish. Let cool.

3 Preheat the oven to 300°F (150°C).

4 Whisk together the eggs, milk, and condensed milk in a large mixing bowl. Put the roasting pan with the baking dish into the oven. With the door open, carefully and gently pour the milk mixture over the caramel in the baking dish. Pour enough boiling water into the roasting pan to come halfway up the sides of the baking dish.

5 Bake for 1 hour. The mixture should wobble in the center when tapped gently. Carefully remove the baking dish from the roasting pan. Set aside to cool. Cover with plastic wrap. Refrigerate until completely chilled.

6 Gently run a knife along the edges of the baking dish to release the custard from the sides. Invert the crème caramel onto a platter with a lip to catch the caramel. Gently cut into 12 equal pieces. Serve topped with fresh cherries.

TIPS

• You can omit the cherries if you prefer, or serve with a different fresh seasonal fruit of your choice.

• The crème caramel can be made up to a day ahead. Keep it covered in the fridge until ready to serve.

Prosecco "jellies" with cherries and berries

SET | PREP + COOK TIME **30 MINUTES + COOLING + OVERNIGHT REFRIGERATION** | SERVES **6**

Including Prosecco in your gelatin gives a grown-up, modern touch to a retro dessert. The wine's floral notes work particularly well with fresh berries. Unflavored powdered gelatin lets the flavor of the wine shine through and allows you to control the amount of sugar you add.

You will need to start this recipe a day ahead

1 bottle (750ml) regular or rosé Prosecco

2 cups sugar

2 cups fresh cherries, pitted

8 tsp powdered unflavored gelatin

1lb (450g) fresh strawberries

4oz (125g) fresh raspberries

4oz (125g) fresh blueberries

cooking oil spray

2 tsp powdered sugar, sifted

1 Stir the Prosecco and sugar in a large saucepan over high heat until the sugar dissolves. Bring to a boil. Add the cherries; reduce the heat to low. Simmer, covered, for 3 minutes.

2 Meanwhile, sprinkle the gelatin over 1 cup water in a small heatproof bowl. Let stand for 1 minute. Put the bowl in a medium saucepan of simmering water. Stir until the gelatin is dissolved.

3 Transfer the cherry mixture to a large bowl. Stir in the gelatin mixture. Let cool slightly. Refrigerate for 30 minutes or until cooled but not set. Remove from the fridge.

4 Reserve 9oz (250g) of the strawberries, 10 raspberries, and 2 tablespoons blueberries. Hull and halve the remaining strawberries. Combine with the remaining raspberries and blueberries.

5 Lightly spray six 1-cup (250ml) jelly molds with oil. Pour 2 tablespoons of the jelly into each mold. Divide a quarter of the berries among the molds. Refrigerate for 30 minutes or until set. Add the remaining jelly and berries; the molds will not be full. Refrigerate overnight until set.

6 Turn out the jellies onto 6 serving plates (wipe the outsides of the molds with a warm cloth first, to help release the jellies). Garnish with the reserved sliced strawberries, blueberries, and raspberries, dusted with the sifted icing sugar.

TIP

To make 1 large jelly, increase the amount of strawberries used to 1½lb (750g) in total. Lightly spray a 10-cup (2.5l) bowl or mold with oil. Pour 1 cup of the jelly into the bowl. Add a quarter of the berries. Refrigerate for 30 minutes or until set. Add the remaining jelly and berries to the mold. Refrigerate overnight.

Sponge candy and hazelnut frozen parfait

SET | PREP + COOK TIME **50 MINUTES + OVERNIGHT STANDING + FREEZING** | SERVES **8**

This recipe retains all the flavors of a traditional steamed Christmas pudding, but with a refreshing frozen twist. It is spectacular enough to be the centerpiece of a festive meal—at the very least, be sure to serve it at the table for best effect.

You will need to start this recipe 2 days ahead

1 cup glazed mixed fruit

¼ cup glazed or candied cherries

¼ cup golden raisins

¼ cup brandy

4 large eggs, separated, yolks lightly beaten

½ cup powdered sugar

¼ cup cocoa

2oz (55g) dark chocolate (70% cocoa)

⅓ cup roasted hazelnuts, coarsely chopped

2oz (55g) chocolate-dipped sponge candy (see page 114)

2 tsp powdered unflavored gelatin

1 tbsp hot water

1 cup heavy cream

1 cup white chocolate baking chips

red currants, to garnish

1 Put the glazed mixed fruit into a food processor fitted with a metal blade. Process for 3 seconds. Add the glazed cherries; process for 2 seconds. (The fruit chunks should not be too large, or they will tear the dessert when it is cut.) Put the fruit in a medium bowl; add the golden raisins. Stir in the brandy. Cover; store in a cool, dark place overnight.

2 Line an 8-cup (2l) bowl or fluted cake pan with plastic wrap, smoothing the wrap to remove as many wrinkles as possible.

3 Using an electric mixer, beat the egg whites in a small bowl until firm peaks form. Gradually beat in the combined sifted powdered sugar and cocoa. Gradually beat in the lightly beaten egg yolks.

4 Put the dark chocolate in a medium heatproof bowl over a saucepan of simmering water. Stir the chocolate until smooth. Let cool for 5 minutes. Stir the melted chocolate into the egg mixture. Pour the egg-chocolate mixture over the fruit; mix well. Stir in the hazelnuts and the sponge candy, broken into pieces.

5 Sprinkle gelatin over 1 tablespoon hot water in a small heatproof bowl. Put the small bowl in a larger bowl, fill large bowl with boiling water, and stir until gelatin dissolves. Let cool slightly. Stir into chocolate mixture.

6 Using an electric mixer, beat the cream in a small bowl until firm peaks form. Fold into the chocolate mixture. Pour the mixture into the lined bowl or cake pan. Smooth the top. Cover; freeze overnight.

7 To serve, invert the parfait onto a chilled serving plate. Peel away the plastic wrap. Return to the freezer.

8 Put the white chocolate in a medium heatproof bowl over a saucepan of simmering water (don't let the water touch the base of the bowl). Stir the chocolate until smooth. Let cool for 5 minutes, then spoon the chocolate gently over the top of the parfait. Return to the freezer immediately to let the chocolate set. Garnish with red currants and serve.

Florentine-topped fruitcake

BAKED | PREP + COOK TIME **3 HOURS + OVERNIGHT STANDING** | SERVES **20**

Fruitcakes sometimes raise eyebrows. This moist and tender version will completely change your mind about how good they can taste, especially with its Florentine topping, which adds a crunchy contrast. This is a cake worthy of celebrating the festive season.

You will need to start this recipe a day ahead

3 cups golden raisins

1 cup coarsely chopped glazed, candied cherries

1½ cups coarsely chopped pitted dates

¾ cup coarsely chopped dried apricots

½ cup brandy

1 cup butter, room temperature, plus extra for greasing

1 cup firmly packed light brown sugar

1 tbsp finely grated orange zest

5 eggs

½ cup almond flour

1¾ cups flour

1 tsp cinnamon

½ tsp each of allspice and nutmeg

Florentine topping

6 tbsp butter, chopped

⅓ cup firmly packed light soft brown sugar

¼ cup light corn syrup

1 cup flaked almonds

¾ cup glazed cherries, halved

½ cup chopped glazed lemon and orange rind

TIP

- Substitute the dried and glacé fruits with any of your favourites. Keep the weight/quantity the same.
- The cake can be made up to a month ahead. Store at room temperature in an airtight container.

1 Combine the fruit and brandy in a large bowl. Cover. Let stand overnight, stirring occasionally, until the brandy is absorbed.

2 Preheat the oven to 325°F (160°C). Line the bottom and sides of a deep 9in (22cm) cake pan or springform pan with four layers of parchment paper, extending the edges 2in (5cm) above the pan. This will prevent the cake from baking unevenly and burning before the center is baked.

3 Using an electric mixer, beat the butter, sugar, and orange zest in a medium bowl until just combined. Add the eggs, one at a time, beating between additions. (The mixture may appear curdled at this stage, but will come together later.) Stir the egg mixture into the fruit mixture, then stir in the almond flour, flour, cinnamon, allspice, and nutmeg. Mix well.

4 Spoon the mixture evenly into the prepared cake pan. Tap the pan on the countertop to remove any air bubbles. Smooth the surface with damp fingers.

5 Bake the cake for 1 hour 40 minutes.

6 Meanwhile, to make the Florentine topping, melt the butter in a small saucepan over low heat. Add the sugar and corn syrup. Cook, stirring, until the sugar dissolves. Remove from the heat. Stir in the almonds, glazed cherries, and glazed lemon and orange rind

7 Spread the Florentine topping evenly over the top of the cake. Bake for 40 minutes longer or until golden brown and a toothpick inserted into the center comes out clean. (If the Florentine topping starts to over-brown during baking, loosely cover the cake with foil.) Place a piece of parchment paper over the top of the cake, then cover the hot cake tightly with foil. Let cool in the pan overnight.

Cherry and amaretti ice cream log

FROZEN | PREP + COOK TIME **35 MINUTES + FREEZING** | SERVES **8**

This frozen fruit-and-nut-filled dessert is replete with the divine flavors of amaretti cookies and fresh cherries. Instead of cherries, you can use another type of fresh fruit, such as blueberries, raspberries, or blackberries.

You will need to start this recipe a day ahead

5oz (150g) gingersnaps or crunchy ginger cookies

3 tbsp butter, melted (see tips)

8oz (225g) fresh cherries

¼ cup cherry liqueur or Amaretto, divided

5oz (150g) amaretti cookies, crushed, divided

1 x 14oz (396g) can sweetened condensed milk

16oz (450g) crème fraiche

1 tsp vanilla extract

⅓ cup crystallized ginger, chopped (see tips)

1 Grease a 3in x 13in/9-cup (8cm x 33cm/2.25l) straight-sided loaf pan or terrine mold. Line the bottom and sides with plastic wrap or parchment paper.

2 In a food processor, pulse the gingersnaps into fine crumbs. Add the butter and process until just combined. Press the crumb mixture evenly over the bottom of the pan. Freeze while preparing the ice cream.

3 Freeze half of the cherries to use as garnish. Remove the pits from the remaining cherries. Coarsely chop. Put the chopped cherries in a large bowl. Add 1 tablespoon of the liqueur and two-thirds of the crushed amaretti cookies. Let stand.

4 Using an electric mixer, whisk together the condensed milk, crème fraîche, vanilla, and remaining liqueur in a bowl for 5 minutes or until thick. Gently fold the cream mixture into the cherry mixture. Fold in half of the crystallized ginger. Pour over the gingersnap base; flatten the surface. Cover tightly with plastic wrap. Freeze for at least 6 hours or overnight until firm.

5 Remove the ice cream log from the pan, placing it on a cold platter. Serve topped with the frozen cherries, the remaining crystallized ginger, and the remaining amaretti cookies.

TIPS

- Different brands of ginger cookies contain varying amounts of butter, so you may need to increase the amount of butter if the crumbs do not hold together in step 2.
- You can swap chopped dark chocolate for the crystallized ginger, if you like.
- This dessert can be made up to 1 week ahead.

Bourbon, peach, and caramel spiced trifle

SET | PREP + COOK TIME **45 MINUTES + REFRIGERATION** | SERVES **10**

Dulce de leche, the thick caramel, is used here in a twist on the traditional trifle. Grilled peaches replace summer berries, while the whiskey syrup and spiced custard lend an autumnal feel. You can avoid the alcohol by replacing the Bourbon with juice.

2lb (900g) premade pound cake, cut into 1in (2.5cm) cubes

^{2}/$_3$ cup Bourbon whiskey (see tips)

^{1}/$_3$ cup honey

1½lb (750g) ripe peaches, pitted and cut into wedges (see tips)

1 x 13.4oz (380g) can dulce de leche

1^1/$_2$ cups pecans, toasted, coarsely chopped (see tips)

spiced custard cream

2^1/$_2$ cups heavy cream

1^1/$_2$ cups premade vanilla pudding

1^1/$_2$ tbsp honey

1 tsp ground cinnamon

^{1}/$_4$ tsp allspice

^{1}/$_4$ tsp nutmeg

1 Arrange the pound cake in the bottom of an 18-cup (4.5l) bowl or dish, cutting to fit. Combine the whiskey, honey, and 2 tablespoons of boiling water in a small bowl. Drizzle ^{1}/$_3$ cup of the whiskey mixture over the cake. Transfer the remaining whiskey mixture to a small saucepan over high heat. Bring to a boil. Simmer for 10–15 minutes or until reduced by half. Let cool.

2 Heat a ridged cast iron grill pan over medium-high heat. Grill the peaches, turning, for 2 minutes or until grill marks appear. Transfer to a tray. Refrigerate the peaches until needed.

3 Meanwhile, make the spiced custard cream. Using an electric mixer, beat the heavy cream in a bowl until firm peaks form. Reserve half of the whipped cream. Fold the pudding, honey, and spices through the remaining whipped cream. Cover. Refrigerate until needed.

4 Arrange half of the peaches and their juice over the cake in the bowl. Top with the spiced custard cream and reduced whiskey mixture. Reserve ^{1}/$_3$ cup dulce de leche for serving. Drop spoonfuls of the remaining dulce de leche over the custard. Sprinkle with 1 cup of the pecans. Refrigerate for 15 minutes.

5 Swirl the reserved dulce de leche through the reserved whipped cream. Spoon over the top of the trifle. Top with the remaining peaches and sprinkle with the remaining pecans. Serve.

TIPS

- Use peach or orange juice in place of whiskey, and canned peaches instead of fresh, if you prefer.
- To roast the pecans, spread them on a baking sheet. Roast in the oven at 350°F (180°C) for 5 minutes or until golden brown. Alternatively, put the pecans in a heavy-based skillet and toast over medium heat until fragrant.
- The trifle can be made up to 6 hours ahead and refrigerated until needed.

Grape and dark chocolate panettone loaf

PREP + COOK TIME **1 HOUR 45 MINUTES + STANDING** | SERVES **10**

Like pandoro, panettone is an Italian Christmas specialty, and its popularity has spread around the world. Serve this contemporary variation, in the shape of a loaf, sliced and toasted as dessert for a festive brunch.

$^3/_4$ cup whole milk, lukewarm

$2^1/_4$ tsp (1 packet) dried yeast

1 cup sugar, divided

6 cups bread flour, divided

1 tbsp finely grated orange zest

3 eggs

4 egg yolks

$^3/_4$ cup plus 1 tbsp butter, softened

$^1/_4$ cup finely chopped candied orange peel

1lb (450g) red seedless grapes, such as cotton candy or Champagne, separated into small clusters

$^1/_2$ cup sweet sherry, such as Pedro Ximénez

$^1/_2$ cup fresh orange juice

$1^1/_4$ cups dark chocolate chips

1 egg white, lightly beaten

2 tbsp demerara sugar

1 Combine the milk, yeast, and 1 tablespoon of the sugar in a small bowl. Let stand for 5 minutes or until slightly frothy on top.

2 Put the remaining sugar, $1^1/_2$ cups of the flour, the yeast mixture, and orange zest in the large bowl of an electric mixer fitted with a dough hook. Mix on low speed for 4 minutes or until smooth and elastic.

3 Add the eggs, egg yolks, butter, and remaining flour. Mix on medium speed for 8 minutes or until smooth, glossy, and elastic. Add the candied orange peel. Mix until just combined. Transfer to a lightly greased large bowl. Cover with lightly greased plastic wrap. Let stand in a warm place for $3^1/_2$ hours or until doubled in size.

4 Meanwhile, put the grapes, sherry, and orange juice in a small saucepan, ensuring the grapes are covered by the liquid. Bring to a simmer over high heat. Cook for 3 minutes or until the grapes begin to look glossy. Remove the grapes with a slotted spoon and place in a heatproof bowl. Continue simmering the liquid for 8 minutes or until syrupy and reduced by one-third. Remove from the heat. Let cool.

5 Preheat the oven to 400°F (200°C). Grease a 4in x 11in (11cm x 27cm) straight-sided loaf pan that's 4in (10cm) deep. Line it with parchment paper, extending the paper 2in (5cm) above the edges of the pan.

6 Turn out the dough onto a clean work surface. Flatten into an 11in (28cm) round. Sprinkle evenly with chocolate. Roll up firmly into a loaf, tucking the ends underneath. Place, seam-side down, in the lined pan. Brush the top of the dough with egg white; sprinkle with demerara sugar. Top with a quarter of the grapes. Let stand for 30 minutes until risen.

7 Bake for 30 minutes, then cover with foil. Reduce the oven temperature to 350°F (180°C). Bake 40–50 minutes longer or until risen and golden. Cool in the pan for 15 minutes. Lift the loaf out of the pan using the parchment paper; place on a wire rack to cool completely. Serve the panettone in slices with the syrup and remaining grapes.

TIP

Panettone is best eaten on the day it was baked, or within 2 days. Store any leftovers in an airtight container. Leftover panettone can be enjoyed sliced and toasted, and it makes excellent French toast.

Eggnog Bavarian cream cake

BAKED | PREP + COOK TIME **45 MINUTES + REFRIGERATION + FREEZING** | SERVES **10**

A touch of cinnamon, nutmeg, and clove in the Bavarian cream makes this dessert seasonal, but it is hard to resist at any time of the year. And what a show-stopper! Look for blends of fancy cake decorating sugars in metallic colors to brighten up the garnish.

4 cups premade vanilla pudding, divided

1/3 cup dark rum

1/3 cup sugar

1 tsp vanilla extract

1 tsp ground nutmeg

3/4 tsp ground cinnamon

1/2 tsp ground cloves

2 titanium-strength gelatin sheets

1 recipe (2 rounds) of Stacked Mocha Blackout Cake (see page 82 and see tips)

1 1/4 cup heavy cream

chocolate trees

1 cup dark chocolate chips, melted

2 tsp chocolate sugar pearls (dragées)

gold sanding sugar

star-shaped candies

rum butterscotch sauce

1 cup firmly packed light brown sugar

1 1/4 cups heavy cream

4 tbsp butter, chopped

1 tbsp dark rum

TIPS

• The cake and sauce can both be made a day ahead and refrigerated. If the sauce separates, stir well to bring it back together before serving.

• Let the cake and sauce stand at room temperature for 45 minutes before serving.

1 Place 2 cups of the vanilla pudding, the rum, sugar, vanilla, and spices in a medium saucepan. Bring to a boil, whisking until the sugar dissolves. Simmer for 2 minutes. Remove from the heat.

2 Put the gelatin in a bowl of cold water for 5 minutes until softened. Squeeze excess water from the gelatin; add the sheets to the hot custard mixture. Stir until dissolved. Transfer to a large heatproof bowl. Whisk in the remaining pudding. Let stand for 5 minutes until cool.

3 Grease a 6in (15cm) springform pan that's 6in (15cm) deep and line the bottom with parchment paper. Trim the tops of the cakes to level them, and trim the sides to ensure they fit in the pan. Then cut each round in half horizontally to make 4 cake rounds. Reserve the trimmings. Place a first layer in the bottom of the cake pan.

4 Beat the cream in a medium bowl until medium peaks form. Fold in the vanilla pudding mixture. Working quickly, pour 1 cup of the mixture over the cake in the pan. Top with another layer of cake. Repeat layering the remaining cream and cake layers, finishing with the last portion of cream over the top. Use a small spatula to level the surface. Tap the pan on the counter to remove air bubbles. Cover. Refrigerate at least 4 hours.

5 Meanwhile, make the rum butterscotch sauce. Combine the ingredients in a small heavy-based saucepan. Bring to a boil, stirring, until the sugar dissolves. Simmer for 5 minutes or until the sauce thickens. Let cool. Refrigerate until cold and thick.

6 Place 3 bamboo skewers or wooden stir sticks on a baking sheet lined with parchment paper. Put the melted chocolate in a piping bag. Snip off the end of the piping bag. Pipe tree shapes halfway up the skewers. Decorate with sugar pearls, sanding sugar, and stars. Freeze until firm.

7 Remove collar from pan and transfer the cake to a serving plate. Insert the trees into the top. Crumble some of the reserved cake trimmings around the tree "trunks." Serve with the rum butterscotch sauce.

Conversion chart

A note on Australian measures

- One Australian metric measuring cup holds approximately 250ml.

- One Australian metric tablespoon holds 20ml.

- One Australian metric teaspoon holds 5ml.

- The difference between one country's measuring cups and another's is within a two- or three-teaspoon variance, and should not affect your cooking results.

- North America, New Zealand, and the United Kingdom use a 15ml tablespoon.

Using measures in this book

- All cup and spoon measurements are level.

- The most accurate way of measuring dry ingredients is to weigh them.

- When measuring liquids, use a clear glass or plastic jug with metric markings.

- We use large eggs with an average weight of 60g. Fruit and vegetables are assumed to be medium unless otherwise stated.

Dry measures

metric	imperial
15g	$^1/_2$oz
30g	1oz
60g	2oz
90g	3oz
125g	4oz ($^1/_4$lb)
155g	5oz
185g	6oz
220g	7oz
250g	8oz ($^1/_2$lb)
280g	9oz
315g	10oz
345g	11oz
375g	12oz ($^3/_4$lb)
410g	13oz
440g	14oz
470g	15oz
500g	16oz (1lb)
750g	24oz (1$^1/_2$lb)
1kg	32oz (2lb)

Liquid measures

metric	imperial
30ml	1 fluid oz
60ml	2 fluid oz
100ml	3 fluid oz
125ml	4 fluid oz
150ml	5 fluid oz
190ml	6 fluid oz
250ml	8 fluid oz
300ml	10 fluid oz
500ml	16 fluid oz
600ml	20 fluid oz
1000ml (1 litre)	1$^3/_4$ pints

Length measures

metric	imperial
3mm	$^1/_8$in
6mm	$^1/_4$in
1cm	$^1/_2$in
2cm	$^3/_4$in
2.5cm	1in
5cm	2in
6cm	2$^1/_2$in
8cm	3in
10cm	4in
13cm	5in
15cm	6in
18cm	7in
20cm	8in
22cm	9in
25cm	10in
28cm	11in
30cm	12in (1ft)

Oven temperatures

The oven temperatures in this book are for conventional ovens; if you have a convection oven, decrease the temperature by 10–20 degrees.

°F (Fahrenheit)	°C (Celsius)
250	120
300	150
325	160
350	180
400	200
425	220
475	240

Index

Acknowledgments

DK would like to thank Sophia Young, Joe Reville, Amanda Chebatte, and Georgia Moore for their assistance in making this book.

The Australian Women's Weekly Test Kitchen in Sydney has developed, tested, and photographed the recipes in this book.